Understanding Freud

UNDERSTANDING FREUD

The Man and His Ideas

Edited by
Emanuel E. Garcia

NEW YORK UNIVERSITY PRESS
New York and London

NEW YORK UNIVERSITY PRESS
New York and London

Copyright © 1992 by New York University

Library of Congress Cataloging-in-Publication Data

Understanding Freud : the man and his ideas / edited by Emanuel E.
   Garcia.
      p.   cm.
   Papers presented at a symposium, held in Philadelphia on 22 Sept.,
1990 and sponsored by the Freud Literary Heritage Foundation.
   Includes bibliographical references and index.
   ISBN 0-8147-3045-0
   1. Freud, Sigmund, 1856–1939—Congresses. 2. Psychoanalysis—
History—Congresses.   I. Garcia, Emanuel E., 1954–   .
BF109.F74U53   1992
150.19'52—dc20   92-4146
                              CIP

New York University Press books are printed on acid-free paper,
and their binding materials are chosen for strength and durability.

Manufactured in the United States of America

c 10 9 8 7 6 5 4 3 2 1

Contents

Acknowledgments

Without the help and encouragement of Dr. Layton McCurdy, formerly the Psychiatrist-in-Chief of the Institute of Pennsylvania Hospital in Philadelphia, the symposium "Understanding Freud" and hence this book would not have been possible. He has my deepest gratitude for his efforts.

Other members of the Institute of Pennsylvania Hospital staff also deserve commendation for their work on the symposium, namely, Jane Century, Susanne Kern, and June Strickland. Olivia Rheinhart's unflagging energy and organizational ability were indispensable and are especially appreciated.

I would like also to thank the Philadelphia Association for Psychoanalysis, the Philadelphia Psychoanalytic Society, and the Institute for Psychoanalytic Psychotherapies (Philadelphia) for their role in suggesting representative members as symposium discussants. Their work now fills these pages.

I am indebted to Jason Renker and to the excellent and receptive staff of New York University Press, with whom it has been a pleasure to work.

Finally, I want to bring to the reader's attention that the abbreviation *S.E.* means that references come from *The Standard Edition of the Complete Psychological Works of Sigmund Freud,* translated and under the general editorship of James Strachey in collaboration with Anna Freud. London: Hogarth Press and the Institute of Psycho-Analysis, 24 vols. (1953–74).

E.E.G.

Contributors

Howard H. Covitz is Associate Director of the Institute for Psychoanalytic Psychotherapies in Philadelphia and is on the Mathematics Faculty, Villanova University.

K. R. Eissler, M.D., is a Member of the New York Psychoanalytic Society, the American Psychoanalytic Association, and the International Psychoanalytical Association.

Elio J. Frattaroli, M.D. is Clinical Assistant Professor of Psychiatry, University of Pennsylvania School of Medicine, and Associate Faculty of the Institute of the Philadelphia Association for Psychoanalysis.

Emanuel E. Garcia, M.D., is Associate Psychiatrist, The Institute of Pennsylvania Hospital, Candidate, Philadelphia Association for Psychoanalysis, and Clinical Associate in Psychiatry, Hospital of the University of Pennsylvania.

Albrecht Hirschmüller, M.D., is Privatdozent, Institute for the History of Medicine, Tübingen, Germany, and is an Analytic Psychotherapist.

Robert A. Paul, Ph.D., is Charles Howard Candler Professor of Anthropology, Graduate Institute of the Liberal Arts, Emory University.

George H. Pollock, M.D., Ph.D., is Ruth and Evelyn Dunbar Distinguished Professor of Psychiatry and Behavioral Sciences, Northwestern University Medical School.

Albert J. Solnit, M.D., is Sterling Professor of Pediatrics and Psychiatry, and Coordinator, Muriel Gardiner Program in Psychoanalysis and the Humanities, Yale University.

Thomas S. Wolman, M.D., is Clinical Assistant Professor of Psychiatry and Human Behavior, Jefferson Medical College, and Associate Member, Philadelphia Psychoanalytic Society.

Clifford Yorke, FRC Psych., D.P.M. is Psychiatrist-in-Charge at the Anna Freud Centre, London.

Foreword

Clifford Yorke

The reputation and status of Freud in the contemporary world is utterly unlike that of any other man of genius. People who know nothing of Dante, Goethe, or Newton will hesitate to express opinions on either their lives or work; people who know nothing of Freud will not only do so without blushing—they will *write* about him as well. Nor do they have difficulty finding an audience. Year by year books *about* Freud, many without any stamp of authority, multiply as if by geometric progression. Books *by* Freud on the other hand, remain largely unread.

The contemporary position has, I believe, its counterpart in a modern myth: that Freud has had a decisive influence on the twentieth century. The evidence for this seems decidedly thin. Proper Freudiana bears at best an insubstantial relationship to what Freud really said. It is one thing to call attention to slips of the tongue, childhood sexuality (without taking it too seriously), and the possible significance of dreams. It is quite another to say that basic Freudian principles are in any real sense understood.

The fact that the reader of Freud in English is particularly well served has not led people to buy his books in droves. Strachey's superbly edited translation of the complete psychological works will be found in reputable libraries, but is widely read mostly by scholars. That is understandable. But attractively produced and inexpensive selections, free of the detailed footnotes and cross references demanded by the committed student, and aimed at the man in the street, sell selectively rather than uniformly. And it seems worth recalling that the lack of interest in what Freud really *says* is nothing new. *The Interpretation of Dreams* took six years to sell the first 350 copies, and *Three Essays on the Theory of Sexuality* did not do much better. Although it was received with outrage, branded its author a pervert in the minds of many, and might on that account have been expected to achieve a *succés de scandale*, the first edition—1,000 copies of a cheap paperback—was still not sold out after four years in print. In that respect, nothing has changed very much. For that matter, I would even question the assumption that professional psychoanalysts must have thoroughly read their Freud. My own experience of psychoanalytic training institutes suggests that, if qualification depended on an examination that required, whatever else, a reasonably thorough knowledge of his work, the majority of students would fail.

An appreciation of Freud and of his contribution to our knowledge of the way the mind works demands more than familiarity with his writings. The serious student in English will complement his reading of the Standard Edition with Ernest Jones's signed biography. It convincingly relates the life to the work in a way that has not been equaled by any other biographer. And in Freud's case this relationship is of capital importance. The late Walker Kaufmann has convincingly demonstrated, in an argument elegantly set out in his book *Discovering the Mind*, that Freud's greatness as a human being was itself a major contributor to his discoveries. To traduce him is to diminish his achievements. Kaufmann attempts to answer the question: What *kind* of mind is needed for discovering the mind? He finds that Freud was uniquely equipped to do so.

The student of Freud is also indebted to another major work: *The Origins of Psychoanalysis. Letters to Wilhelm Fliess, Draft and Notes: 1887–1902*, edited by Marie Bonaparte, Anna Freud, and

Ernst Kris. The letters and notes demonstrate, as perhaps nothing else can, the mind of genius in action, in the throes of its own creativity.

This serves to remind us that scholarly editions of Freud's letters are urgently called for. It is this onerous task that the Freud Literary Heritage Foundation has set out to further. The importance of these letters is repeatedly demonstrated in the present work, for example by Dr. Garcia in his essays and by Dr. Kurt Eissler in his fine contribution. But what the reader now has before him is a work of scholarship by people who love the man and the work and who strive tirelessly to foster a wider awareness of both.

Introduction

Emanuel E. Garcia

The chapters in this volume were presented at a symposium entitled "Understanding Freud," which was held on 22 September 1990 in Philadelphia, a day before the fifty-first anniversary of Freud's death in London. These essays need no further introduction: they represent attempts to come to grips with Freud's work and with the creative processes of his mind that characterized his genius.

I would like to offer my own condensed summary of Freud's achievements, and then to comment on some of their under-appreciated consequences. First and foremost, Freud was able to describe, in a way that no one had hitherto been able to accomplish, *how the mind actually works.* He showed that mental activity could be organized according to the operation of basic principles and mechanisms, for example, wish fulfillment, the pleasure principle, condensation, displacement, symbolism and other means of representation, projection, overdetermination, regression, repression, defense, primary and secondary processes, and the division of the mind into the realms of consciousness and the unconscious. To do this he took the giant step of refuting the assumed equation of psyche and consciousness. In a magnificent passage, to which volumes could be devoted, Freud wrote: "The unconscious is the true psychical reality; *in its innermost nature it is as much unknown to us as the reality of the external world, and it is as incompletely presented by the data of consciousness as is the external world by the communications of our sense organs*" (1900, 613; Freud's emphasis). For Freud the unconscious is not a static domain reducible to formulaic rules and facile modes of expression: it is a mysterious and ultimately unknowable region characterized by ceaseless flux, exerting the dominant motivating forces of behavior.

Second, Freud contravened the accumulated wisdom of ages by establishing the inestimable importance of the early years of life on all later individual and societal development, demonstrating how complex and powerful are the influences of pleasure, that is, of childhood sexuality. Furthermore, by demystifying and destigmatizing sexuality, he granted both male and female the potential for liberating themselves not only from repressive cultural attitudes toward sex, but from the unconscious dictatorship of infantile sexual imperatives.

Third, Freud created a reliable method for investigating the unconscious via the technique of free association. What the poets divined by the flash of inspiration Freud could set about uncovering and organizing relatively systematically.

Fourth, he devised a psychological treatment that was incomparable in its ability to foster self-understanding, and the treatment setting itself became a historically novel institution predicated on complete confidentiality and frankness of expression as no other human situation had been.

Fifth, he showed how analytic discoveries could be relevantly applied to all facets of the human experience and its study—the arts, religion, medicine, anthropology, psychiatry, civilization, biology, phylogeny, group behavior, and cultural history. He himself pioneered the application of analytic research to these fields, and it is here that analysis nowadays may be able to make its most valuable contributions.

Sixth, he created a humanistic revolution by abolishing the hitherto unbridgeable division between the psychologically abnormal from the normal and showing the common roots of dreams, hysteria, jokes, slips of the tongue, obsessional ideas, paranoia, and so forth. No longer could the mentally afflicted, the neurotic or psychotic, be dismissed as some qualitatively different and despised subspecies of humanity.

Some aspects of this phenomenal legacy have attracted little notice, and may be best introduced by reference to a passage Freud wrote to Hugo Heller, a Viennese bookseller who asked Freud to name "ten good books." In his reply to Heller, Freud (1907) linked Copernicus, Darwin, and Johann Weyer as authors of the three most significant books in history. I have argued elsewhere (Garcia 1989) that Freud's mention of Weyer—the only known instance in the Standard Edition or in his published correspondence—effectively established a link between the work of Weyer and that of psychoanalysis in Freud's mind.

Weyer, the so-called father of modern psychiatry, courageously opposed the Inquisition's view of mental illness as evidence of sorcery, denounced its cruelties and ignorance, and conducted empiric investigations that emphasized natural explanations for many of the ostensibly supernaturally induced psychic phenomena (Weyer 1583). For example, the old woman whom the Inquisitors were so eager to burn at the stake because she claimed to have caused an epidemic among cattle or to have created harsh weather was revealed by Weyer to be suffering from delusional melancholia. Mere words, ideas, delusions given voice by "witches"—these were not, according to Weyer, to be equated with deeds, and hence could not be punishable as such. This attitude marked a tremendous advance for humanity in its destruction of the illusion of omnipotence of thought, a blow against human megalomania that presaged the wound to mankind's narcissism, which psychoanalysis delivered by recognizing that the ego is not even master in its own house.

The fact that thoughts are not deeds is central to psychoanalysis, though it runs against the grain of accepted opinion and common daily practice, particularly as promulgated by the Catholic religion, which in its tally of sinfulness and for purposes of penance sees no such distinction. One recalls Little Hans's confession of his oedipal wishes to his father, possibly the first time a child had done so without fear of retribution in accordance with the *lex talionis*—a confession that was made possible only by the freedom of expression implicit in the psychoanalytic setting. But even the father of Little Hans fell into the practice of condemning mere thought, like the Inquisitors. When Little Hans expressed his wish that his sister would die, his father attempted to convince him that a good boy should not wish that sort of thing (Freud 1909, 72). Hans, however, earned Freud's high praise by defending his right to think whatever he pleased. Freud remarked, "I could wish for no better understanding of psycho-analysis from any grown-up" (1909, 72).

There may yet come a day when the liberty to accept any fantasy, no matter how repulsive, abhorrent, or fearful, without guilt or anxiety, will be the rule. The consequent widening of the scope of ego function in the individual and society may lead to undreamed of possibilities for civilization. This indeed would be a great triumph for psychoanalysis, though the likelihood of such a course is very small.

The world today is a dangerous place. Knowing full well that I risk falling into the trap of overvaluing the uniqueness of our times, I believe that the collective and individual burdens upon humankind have never been greater. Today's technological and scientific capabilities are truly awe-inspiring—I am thinking particularly of the triumphs of genetic research, space exploration, and telecommunications—and they have resulted in achievements that were unimaginable to our ancestors. For example, live events from nearly every nook and cranny of the planet can now be visualized in one's home as a matter of routine, across all economic classes: even the poorest households in America possess televisions. Yet the massive social problems of our day—war, the inequitable distribution of resources, overpopulation, the destruction of the environment, nationalism, nuclear weaponry—seem impervious to solution.

We find ourselves in the midst of a cultural habitat for which we are poorly equipped. The evolutionary forces that shaped and molded the bipedal mammal that became *Homo sapiens* are now obsolete: cultural evolution has taken over. The discordance between the claims of our biological heritage and our new cultural calling has widened. As one scholar has put it, "People with the motivations and intellectual capacity of late upper paleolithic man are now flying jet bombers and confronted with the task of surviving in anonymous society"(Eibl-Eibesfeldt 1989, 15).

The sheer numbers of people in any modern society present insuperable difficulties to the individual, whose cognitive endowment is not furnished with an ability to conceptualize more than a few hundred objects in a personally meaningful way. Ideas of hundreds of thousands, or millions, of persons are accommodated only through the obliterative work of condensation. Thus the formation of groups that are themselves identifiable in a sea of anonymity and yet can offer the solace of productive and meaningful roles for individuals within is essential. In light of this, would it not be wise to consult Freud's *Group Psychology and the Analysis of the Ego* as a blueprint for the comprehension of the individual's relation to larger entities, of the personal characteristics of leaders who appeal to the masses, of the types and kinds of manipulation that can be practiced and of the functioning of the group psyche? Would it not be helpful to consult *Civilization and Its Discontents* for an understanding of the source of modern man's restlessness, and a potential solution? Or to read *Moses and Monotheism* to appreciate the evolution of cultural identities and the unconscious forces of history that inform current action? It is my belief that Freud's ideas are essential for allowing society to overcome the obstacles that threaten its very survival. Like the conundrum posed by Freud's self-analysis, the issue writ large is to ascertain how the group psyche can avert disaster by transcending inherent and seemingly insuperable limitations.

Let me return from the ambitious topic of societal existence to the more manageable one of Freud's life. Fortunately for us, Freud was a voluminous correspondent. He poured himself into his letters, charting with illuminating verve and ruthless honesty the vicissitudes of spirit that accompanied his life's struggles. They complement the Standard Edition to give an extraordinary portrait of human experience rivaled in its depth and breadth only by Shakespeare, Goethe, and a few other surpassing giants.

Far more urgent than the quest for a so-called definitive biography of Freud is the task of editing and publishing the complete correspondence and thus allowing Freud to reveal himself in a way not permitted by the constraints of biography or autobiography. A biographer after all can see no farther into his subject than he can see into himself. Autobiography is handicapped in addition by a limiting reserve that bars the door to personally sensitive material or to facts that do not serve the purpose that inspired its writing. Letters, on the other hand, when they are not written as self-conscious documents for posterity's admiration (and Freud's were certainly not composed in this manner), show the mind in spontaneous unguarded flux grappling with issues of the moment. From Freud's published correspondence alone a rich and unrivaled, though vastly incomplete, biographical record has emerged. One can only wonder what treasures await us in the unpublished material.

A word of caution, however, must be introduced regarding the temptation to rely on private documents to assess scientific ideas. The relevance of Freud's epistolary observations to his published assertions is an extremely tricky and complicated issue. All too easily may one fall into the trap of misapprehension by relying on the letters, for example, as primary evidence in support of this or that hypothesis. Freud's published writings remain the authoritative embodiment of his observations and theories; it was these works which he offered to the public for evaluation in accordance with the scientific method, not the speculative meanderings of his personal letters, stimulating as these meanderings may have been.

Having said this, allow me to cite two letters by Freud that give a sense of the unique intertwining of his personal and scientific sides and thus a glimpse into certain important facets of his character. The first is a letter of 25 May 1916 to Lou Andreas-Salomé, the brilliant author who had been associated with Nietzsche and Rilke before her encounter with Freud and her study and practice of psychoanalysis. Calling Salomé an "understander" par excellence, Freud remarked:

> I am always particularly impressed when I read what you have to say on one of my papers. I know that in writing I have to blind myself artificially in order to focus all the light on one dark spot, renouncing cohesion, harmony, rhetoric and everything which you call symbolic, frightened as I am by the experience that any such claim or expectation involves the danger of

distorting the matter under investigation, even though it may embellish it. Then you come along and add what is missing, build upon it, putting what has been isolated back into its proper context. I cannot always follow you, for my eyes, adapted as they are to the dark, probably can't stand strong light or an extensive range of vision. But I haven't become so much of a mole as to be incapable of enjoying the idea of a brighter light and more spacious horizon, or even to deny their existence. (Pfeiffer 1966, 45)

Even in translation Freud's literary skills are remarkably evident. His imagery is unaffected but striking, effortlessly incorporated without disturbing the tone of mature friendship. He praises Salomé for possessing qualities he admires but lacks—for example, the knack of synthesizing, of creating an overarching framework—but he does not disparage his own highly focused analytic approach. "Psycho-analysis," Freud had written in his history of the field, "has never claimed to provide a complete theory of human mentality in general, but only expected that what it offered should be applied to supplement and correct the knowledge acquired by other means" (1914, 50). Freud was very much at ease with incompleteness. He recognized that all knowledge was fragmentary and shied away from anything resembling the construction of grand philosophical or religious world orders—an attitude that has cost him many an admirer but which is the epitome of scientific realism and a key to comprehending his opus. This letter is a beautiful enunciation of Freud's general epistemological perspective, deep scientific humility, and willing acceptance of the novel and "brighter" contributions of others toward psychoanalysis.

The next letter I wish to highlight was written to Ludwig Binswanger, the Swiss existential psychiatrist with whom Freud enjoyed a long friendship undisturbed by differing theoretical views. Binswanger had informed Freud of the death of his eldest son. In his reply Freud alluded to the untimely death of his own "Sunday child" Sophie nine years before, and then went on to offer the following words of consolation:

Although we know that after such a loss the acute state of mourning will subside, we also know we shall remain inconsolable and will never find a substitute. No matter what may fill the gap, even if it be filled completely, it nevertheless remains something else. And actually this is how it should be. It is the only way of perpetuating that love which we do not want to relinquish. (12 April 1929, in Freud 1960, 386)

All of us at one time or another have been confronted by the task of attempting to assuage the grief of a friend who has lost a loved one. Invariably we find ourselves at a loss. We seek to convey a depth of sympathetic feeling that will show how we have been touched by our friend's sorrow, yet we realize it is peculiarly his or her own, an intensely private matter warranting respect for its unique character. We also secretly are glad that Fate has spared us, and we may be guilty for our escape from calamity. We wish to offer help, but we know full well that the only help the aggrieved desires at the time is the undoing of reality. Our words seem thin, hollow, or overrich, our condolences pitifully inadequate. Our realization of such inadequacy only adds to the bitter taste left by the terrifying demonstration of the utter fragility and unpredictability of existence.

Bringing his analytic acumen into the service of personal emotion, Freud composed a magnificent passage that manages to be both a moving communication of sympathy and a telling set of general observations about the human psyche. He acknowledges the inconsolability of the bereaved, and then goes on to lay bare the motivation for this universal response, namely, preservation of the love of the deceased. The wish-fulfilling aspect of inconsolability is poignantly illuminated by the remarkable comment on the impossibility of substitution, which is reminiscent of his statement in *Mourning and Melancholia* that "people never willingly abandon a libidinal position, not even, indeed, when a substitute is already beckoning to them" (Freud 1917, 244). Yet both the striving for a substitute and the necessary imperishability of human attachments are recognized and alluded to in a phrase of consummate linguistic skill: "No matter what may fill the gap, even if it be filled completely, it nevertheless remains something else." As this example shows, a study of Freud's correspondence purely for its addition to general psychological knowledge would be an immensely rich and challenging undertaking.

I hope that the views I have expressed on the problems and potentials of the study of Freud's life and work will, if anything, encourage the reading and rereading of Freud's writings with an eye toward furthering the science he so laboriously brought into being.

References

Eibl-Eibesfeldt, I. 1989. *Human Ethology*. New York: Aldine de Gruyter.

Eissler, K. R. 1971. *Talent and Genius: The Fictitious Case of Tausk contra Freud*. New York: Quadrangle Books.

Freud, S. 1900. The interpretation of dreams. *S.E.* 4 and 5.

———. 1907. Contributions to a questionnaire on reading. *S.E.* 9:245–247.

———. 1909. Analysis of a phobia in a five-year-old boy. *S.E.* 10:5–147.

———. 1914. On the history of the psycho-analytic movement. *S.E.* 14:7–66.

———. 1917. Mourning and melancholia. *S.E.* 14:243–258.

———. 1960. *Letters of Sigmund Freud*, ed. E. L. Freud. New York: Basic Books.

Garcia, E. E. 1989. Johann Weyer and Sigmund Freud: A psychoanalytic note on science, narcissism and aggression. *American Imago* 46:21–36.

Pfeiffer, E., ed. 1966. *Sigmund Freud and Lou Andreas-Salomé: Letters*. New York: Harcourt Brace Jovanovich.

Weyer, J. 1583. *De praestigiis daemonum*, in G. Mora, *Witches, Devils and Doctors in the Renaissance*. Binghamton, N.Y.: Medieval and Renaissance Texts and Studies, 1991.

1

Freud's Anthropology: A Reading of the "Cultural Books"

Robert A. Paul

How can the insights into individual psychology gained through the techniques of psychoanalysis illuminate the cultural, collective life of people in society? Freud returned to this question throughout his career in a series of works sometimes referred to as the "cultural books." These include *Totem and Taboo* (1913), *Group Psychology and the Analysis of the Ego* (1921), *Civilization and Its Discontents* (1930), and *Moses and Monotheism* (1939). In this essay, I will give an exposition of these works in which I stress their unity, their evolution as psychoanalytic theory itself developed, and what I take to be their central argument. I also intend to show how vital aspects of this central argument may, despite the many difficulties these books present to the contemporary student of society and culture, contribute in powerful ways to our understanding of human social existence.

Reprinted by permission of Cambridge University Press, Cambridge and New York, from *The Cambridge Companion to Freud*, edited by Jerome Neu, 1992.

Before turning to the cultural books themselves, however, I want to begin by drawing attention to the fact that Freud was, from the first, concerned with ordinary cultural life. Of the book-length projects to which he applied himself as soon as he had completed the self-analysis which played so crucial a role in his intellectual development, three were nonclinical accounts of normal phenomena in which are visible the workings of unconscious thought processes, namely, dreams (1900), slips of the tongue (1901), and jokes (1905). The effect of these works is to undermine the very distinction between normal and neurotic and to show that something other than rational, secondary process thought is a normal and essential aspect of all human life.

These three books are certainly "cultural" insofar as they explore aspects of thought, speech, and symbolization shared in the public arena of Western society. They do not, however, explicitly address the question of how human culture and society are constituted in general (though the examination of jokes in particular does involve a fine understanding of the social context and interpersonal strategizing involved in joke telling).

It must also be stressed at the outset that Freud's individual psychology itself was never the isolated, hermetically sealed internal system sometimes caricatured by its detractors. As he writes in the Introduction to *Group Psychology*, "In the individual's mental life someone else is invariably involved, as a model, as an object, as a helper, as an opponent; and so from the very first individual psychology, in this extended but entirely justifiable sense of the words, is at the same time a social psychology as well" (1921, 69).

Furthermore, one may well consider "cultural" Freud's essays on art, literature, and myth, all undeniably cultural phenomena. True, in many instances Freud treats the characters in the work as if they were individuals whose motivations and psychodynamics exemplified clinical insights, while in others, such as in the studies of Leonardo (1910) and Dostoevsky (1928), his attention is focused on the psychology of the artist behind the work. In other instances, however, for example in the work on folklore coauthored with Oppenheim (1911), Freud makes clear that he considers the symbolism of the unconscious encountered in dreams and neurotic symptoms to be embedded in the language permeating public cultural discourse; thus folklore is amenable to interpretation along psycho-analytic lines.

One particular case of such public symbolism in myth deserves special attention because of its centrality and because Freud's position is so often misunderstood. When, in *The Interpretation of Dreams*, discussing the theme of death wishes unconsciously felt by children toward a parent, he alludes to Sophocles's *Oedipus Rex*, it is neither to see the play as a manifestation of Sophocles's psychology, nor yet to examine Oedipus's own supposed motives and psycho-dynamics. It is, rather, to show how the play serves as a collective, publicly constituted fantasy which corresponds to the unconscious incestuous and rivalrous fantasies harbored by each member of the audience as repressed residues of childhood. Those critics who have gloated over the fact that Oedipus himself couldn't have had an Oedipus complex miss the point: *we*, being humans and not fictional characters like Oedipus whose exploits are highly unrealistic, *do* have Oedipus complexes; the play thus serves as what Geertz calls a story people tell about themselves about who they are (1973, 448). In *Oedipus Rex* we schematize and epitomize an aspect of our existence, and from this public text we learn how to understand ourselves and how to make ourselves who we are.

It is my contention that if we read Freud's cultural books, replacing his search for historical origins with a focus on such fantasy schemas—individually experienced but also collectively shared, communicated, and transmitted as symbolic representations and as phylogenetic templates—the main arguments take on persuasive force.

The 1907 essay, "Obsessive Acts and Religious Practices," can be seen as an overture to the cultural books, a first statement of Freud's idea that neurosis and cultural phenomena can usefully be compared. In this paper, Freud points to parallels between the private ceremonials of obsessional neurotics and the ritual observances of religion (and one must assume that he has in mind mainly Catholicism and Judaism). They are similar, first of all, in the sense of guilt that both engender if their performance is neglected; but they differ in that the one is variable from person to person, and private, while the other is stereotyped and collective.

The apparent distinction that the neurotic ritual, unlike the religious one, is meaningless disappears when it is realized that the surface triviality and absurdity of obsessional rituals are the result of displacements and other symbolic distortions of an originally perfectly clear idea (while the majority of religious practitioners actually have no inkling of the deep symbolic meaning of the rituals they perform, either).

Dynamically, Freud argues, the two are similar in being based on the renunciation of instinctual impulses. But they differ as to which instinct it is that is being renounced: whereas in the neurosis it is exclusively the sexual instinct that is suppressed, in religion it is self-seeking, socially harmful instincts. At this relatively early stage in his thinking, Freud maintains that there are two classes of instincts whose opposition is at the root of psychodynamic conflict. One is the sexual instinct, or libido; the other is the class of ego instincts, concerned with the survival of the organism, of which the foremost exemplar is hunger. The ego instincts are selfish in the literal sense, looking out at all times for the welfare of *numero uno;* the libido, by contrast, serves the purposes of the genome and the species by ensuring procreative copulation (though this is far from its only actualization in real life).

In this essay Freud puts forward the pithy formulation that one may describe obsessional neurosis "as an individual religiosity and religion as a universal obsessional neurosis" (1907, 126–127). This, I think, is the essence of his thought about civilization: religion is the neurosis of civilization, the price civilized people pay for the instinctual renunciations demanded of them. Nor is it just any neurosis; it is specifically a neurosis of the obsessive-compulsive type.

One is so used to hearing that Freud developed his ideas through the treatment of hysteria common among the women in his clientele that one may be inclined to forget that by the time he turned his attention to cultural issues he had become considerably more interested in obsessional neurosis. Perhaps some impetus came from his self-analysis, in which he encountered obsessional features in himself. In any event, the only two published complete cases he treated himself were ones he diagnosed as obsessional— the Rat Man (1909b) and the Wolf Man (1918). In one of his great final theoretical works, *Inhibitions, Symptoms and Anxiety,* he says quite explicitly that "obsessional neurosis is unquestionably the most interesting and repaying subject of analytic research" (1926, 113).

Since what is now called "Obsessive-Compulsive Personality Disorder" (but not the more full-fledged "obsessional compulsive neurosis") is typically seen in men more than in women, one might understand Freud's apparent privileging of obsessional psychodynamics in understanding civilization as an expression of his own well-known biases on the matter of the sexes. There is no doubt truth in this view; at the same time, one should bear in mind that the problem of which it is a symptom—male domination and its historical and cross-cultural ubiquity—is also one which Freud's theoretical ideas help to explain. If "civilization" is in some meaningful way to be understood on the model of obsessional dynamics; if, furthermore, these dynamics are typical of men; and if, finally, the qualities of this constellation of conflicts lead to a need for control and the isolation of thought from affect, then this would go a long way toward explaining the enigmatic fact of universal gender inequality. That Freud was not himself free of the neurotic and cultural conditions he was able to diagnose does not invalidate his contribution to the understanding of the conditions in which he, and we, find ourselves.

The link between obsessional neurosis and the intertwined origins of religion, society, and civilized morality is the central theme of Freud's next and most important work on the application of psychoanalysis to the study of culture, namely *Totem and Taboo* (1913). The subtitle of the work—"Some Points of Agreement between the Mental Lives of Savages and Neurotics"—has been enough to poison the atmosphere between anthropologists and psychoanalysts for most of a century now; but once again, we lose more than we gain if we allow the dated and objectionable aspects of the work to blind us to its positive contribution.

Freud accepted the notion then prevalent in the anthropological thinking of his day that cultural history was to be understood as a unilinear progression of higher stages of civilization, and that contemporary non-Western, nonliterate peoples stood "very near to primitive man, far nearer than we do," and that "their mental life must have a peculiar interest for us if we are right in seeing in it a well-preserved picture of an early stage of our own development" (1913, 1). In these assumptions he was no different from the authorities upon whom he relied, including Frazer, Tylor, McLennan, Lang, Marett, and, for that matter, Durkheim (whose *Elementary Forms of the Religious Life* [1912] he consulted without, it seems, having been particularly impressed).

In Freud's own thinking, the parallels he drew between obsession and civilization rested on the assumption that the history of civilization could be compared to a human lifetime, and that the customs of people closer to the childhood of the race could be understood on the analogy of the fantasies, conflicts, and phase-appropriate neuroses of individual childhood. These views are no longer tenable; nonetheless, we must take them as the basis for reading Freud's work and for finding our way toward a more plausible and useful interpretation of what he saw.

The first of the four essays that comprise the work, "The Horror of Incest," shows that Australian aboriginal peoples—"the most backward and miserable of savages"—are not only concerned about regulating sexual life, but go to great lengths to prevent incest. Their marriage rules, section systems, and avoidance customs are the cultural equivalents of the prohibitions on incest enforced in each individual's psyche through the agency of the superego established in the wake of the resolution of the Oedipus complex.

In the second essay, "Taboo and Emotional Ambivalence," the "taboos" of the Polynesians and others are compared with the prohibitions and ceremoniais of obsessional neurosis. Ambivalence, the central dynamic feature of obsessional neurosis, is the situation in which every affectionate relationship is offset by an equal but generally unconscious undercurrent of hostility toward the same person. The prohibitions and rituals of the obsessional are necessary to protect love and the loved ones from danger, which, since it emanates from oneself, is ever present. The primary prohibition is against touching, which originally is understood in the sexual sense as masturbation, but is extended to any sort of contact. The sexual fantasies aroused by masturbation lead to the dread of castration in retaliation for murderous wishes against the Oedipal rival; the sexual and hostile impulses are repressed, but displacement leads to a constant "seepage." The result is the obsessional's fear of contagion, and the preventative measures of isolation, in which thoughts are kept apart from each other and from the feelings appropriate to them (to keep them from "touching").

Freud shows that taboo states in many societies correspond in that taboo people and things are likewise "contagious," through constant displacement. Further, people and situations surrounded by taboo are those likely to evoke selfish and hostile impulses, precisely the ones repressed in the emotional ambivalence of obsessional neurosis.

Having shown the "points of agreement," Freud turns to the differences between ritual taboos and obsessional prohibitions. First, there is still, as in 1907, the difference between the instincts prohibited. In the neurosis, Freud says, it is a sexual impulse that must be controlled (since it brings with it hostile thoughts which are a source of danger). In the case of cultural taboos, the prohibition is on touching not in the sexual sense but "in the more general sense of attacking, or getting control, and of asserting oneself" (1913, 73). The impulses prohibited are, then, a "combination of egoistic and erotic components into wholes of a special kind" (p. 73). What this unique instinctual blend might be will become clearer presently.

A second difference, as in the 1907 paper, is that the neurosis is a "caricature" of a cultural form; neuroses "endeavor to achieve by private means what is effected in society by collective effort" (p. 73). Freud goes further this time, though, and asserts that sexual instincts are unsuited to uniting men in society; *that* job is better done by the demands of self-preservation.

It seems at first contradictory to claim that egoistic instincts should be more suitable for leading people to unite in social groups than libidinal ones. The confusion is, I think, due to the state of flux in which Freud's instinct theory found itself at the time: he was about to jettison the distinction between ego and libidinal instincts altogether and replace them with a single instinct, libido, which could be directed either toward the self or toward an object (1913). The "self-preservative" instincts thus turn out to be *both* "egoistic" and "libidinal." The "whole of a special kind" he had referred to would thus be narcissism, libidinal investment of the self. Social instincts, then, at this point in Freud's thought, are derivatives of narcissistic ones.

The point is elaborated in the third essay, "Animism, Magic and the Omnipotence of Thoughts." Both the "savage" and the obsessional neurotic, Freud argues, act as if they believed that wishes equal deeds, that they can have real effects on the world without any action, and, when they are bad, they can and should be punished like bad deeds. *Ideas* about things, in short, are granted equal value with things themselves. Magic and "animism"—the postulation of an ensouled external world—which are said to typify "primitive" society correspond to the conviction, so typical of obsessional neurotics, that they are as guilty as murderers because of hostile wishes they have harbored, usually unconsciously. The basis of this attitude is the narcissistic overvaluation of one's own psyche and one's power to determine events. In at least part of the mind, the reality principle is rejected as too great a narcissistic blow (since it does not support the illusion of omnipotence); illusory satisfactions and ersatz control are clung to in the neurosis. The constant need for control and defense is required precisely because the neurotic believes he or she is dangerous—a belief resting on the conviction that wishes are deeds.

So far the book has been about "Taboo." In the fourth essay, surely the best known and most notorious, we at last arrive at "Totem"; the essay is called "The Return of Totemism in Childhood." Here Freud proposes to solve what was then—but is certainly no longer—an important anthropological issue, namely, how totemism and exogamy are related, which came first, and under what circumstances. Frazer's four-volume opus *Totemism and Exogamy* was then considered a work of paramount significance (it is now hardly ever read), and scholars struggled to place the two phenomena somewhere in the then accepted universal progression of evolutionary stages thought to characterize the development of religion and society. "Totemism" refers broadly to those ideas according to which certain groups of people are linked with animal species, toward which they must observe some sort of ritual relationship and/or prohibition; "exogamy" refers to the institution whereby one is required to marry a person from outside one's own group (at whatever level that might be defined) and prohibited from marrying within the group. Thus, for example, in contemporary American society the nuclear family is exogamous, in that one may not marry a sibling, parent, or child.

After a conscientious review of the literature (to which the contemporary reader need devote only cursory attention, the debates having long since been completely superseded), Freud proposes his own theory of the origin of both totemism and exogamy. Taking these two features and the prohibitions associated with them to be the main foundations of primordial social life, he wants to show that the injunction not to kill the totem animal, interpreted as a displacement from the father, and the rule not to marry within the group are, respectively, negations of the two great Oedipal wishes; to kill one's father (assuming a male ego here) and "marry" one's mother. The institution of society thus rests on the measures taken to suppress the wishes of the Oedipus complex.

Freud presents his argument as if it emerged from a consideration of three different theories and observations: Darwin's (1871) conception of the original social units in which humans may have lived; Robertson Smith's (1894) theory of the totemic sacrificial feast; and Freud's (1909a) and Ferenczi's (1913) observations of animal phobias in little boys. The last named serve to prove that the totem animal is really the father, since in children, as presumably in "the childhood of the race," animals frequently represent the castrating father around whom phobic ideas nucleate. Robertson Smith's analysis is brought in to show that totem feasts, in which a prohibited animal is killed amid both mourning and rejoicing, are features of the supposed original religion of humankind.

Darwin's contribution to the scenario is his (really quite plausible, if not necessarily correct) suggestion that early humans probably lived in bands composed of a single adult male and those females and their young he was able to control and defend from competitors. The young males would be driven off as soon as they were sexually mature and thus potential rivals; after living a solitary life, they too would, in their turn, establish a mating unit with one or more females. Such an arrangement would, according to Darwin, prevent the dangers of too close inbreeding. (This model is, in fact, a fairly accurate schematic description of gorilla social organization.)

Freud's own theory weaves these strands together to propose that in one fateful era, inaugurating human culture and society, the excluded junior males rebelled against their father, driven by desire for his females, resentment of his tyranny, and new confidence perhaps arising from the possession of some new weapon (I have elsewhere proposed that this new weapon would have been the capacity for culture itself [Paul 1976]). They killed and ate the father, thus by identification gaining some of his authority. The totem meal reenacts this "memorable and criminal deed, which was the beginning of so many things—of social organization, or moral restrictions and of religion" (1913, 142).

Their goal achieved and their hostility spent, the brothers' love for the slain father came to the fore, and in remorse, and through a fear of the war of all against all to which the succession would otherwise lead, they set up the first prohibitions in the name of the now deified patriarch: one must not kill the totem animal (father) and one must not commit what for the first time becomes the crime of "incest" with those very women whose desirability instigated the revolt in the first place, that is, the father's consort(s). The simultaneous sorrow and joy of the totemic feast represent both sides of the ambivalence: the rite both reenacts the triumph and expiates the crime. The prohibition on incest ipso facto inaugurates exogamy and the necessary exchange of wives between groups, while the memory of the dead father becomes the basis for the new moral system, authorized by the guilt felt by the brothers for their act.

Freud suggests that the memory of the original deed has remained in the human unconscious and continues to undergird and enforce human society, which is based on the incest taboo and the collective worship of progressively "higher" deities: first animals, then the hero, then the polytheistic gods, and finally the returned superpatriarch of Judeo-Christian (and Islamic) monotheism. (The matriarchy, then widely believed to have been an important stage in the evolution of society, is slipped rather awkwardly into the interregnum after the father is killed and before the brothers have come to their wits and established civilized social organization.)

Freud's myth of the primal horde has struck a host of observers and critics as far-fetched and overwrought; and certainly, from our point of view, the various arguments based on the assumption of a parallel between the evolution of society and the maturation of an individual—as well as the hypotheses about the matriarchy, the totemic stage of religion, and so on—have lost all but historical interest. It is my contention, however, that behind the melodrama lies the persuasive observation that the Oedipal fantasies of human childhood, based on sexual and aggressive impulses within the nuclear family, have both a cultural and phylogenetic basis, as would be expected given that we evolved under conditions of natural selection for maximum inclusive reproductive fitness. The primal horde probably never existed; but it does ideally embody the *fantasy* of what any male in a sexually reproducing species like ours might *aspire* to in his narcissistic and reproductive self-interest: to father offspring by as many females as possible, and to eliminate all rival males from competition by depriving them—one way or another—of reproductive potential, that is, by "castrating" them.

So well suited for reproduction in social mammals is this arrangement that stockbreeders of herd animals around the world have adopted it as usual practice, as I have pointed out elsewhere (Paul 1982). Breeders re-create the primal horde in their flocks by impregnating all the females with one or a few stud males, and killing and eating, castrating, or subjugating for forced labor the remaining males.

Once we had arrived at the formulation of the primal horde, Freud continued to organize his further thinking about culture and society around it. In his next major cultural work, *Group Psychology and the Analysis of the Ego* (1921), he combines his earlier work on narcissism (1914), his idea of the primal horde, and the new dual instinct theory he had proposed the previous year in *Beyond the Pleasure Principle* (1920). A new instinct theory had been necessary ever since the collapse of the old duality into a unitary view with libido as the only instinctual drive. This situation left libido without an antagonist among the instincts, and thus left Freud at a loss to find a biological underpinning for the endemic conflict he found in human psychology. The new instincts of 1920 are Eros, replacing the old libido; and a new instinct, Thanatos, the drive toward destruction and death.

The latter plays no active role in the *Group Psychology;* the revised version of Eros, however, contributes some new twists to Freud's theory of culture and society. As we saw, sexual love in its pure state leads to transient gratification and cannot form the basis for lasting social bonds. Only erotic impulses that are partly aim-inhibited can transform sexual interest into long-term affectionate love and affiliation. The sexual couple, then, stands in an equivocal midway position between narcissism and group psychology: a pair united in genital love is a self-contained minimal unit, antithetical to the growth of larger units. The primal father himself has been a pure narcissist, in the sense that he gratified every wish, including sexual ones, as soon as it arose. He did not, strictly speaking, lead a social existence in the human sense; even his pairings with his consorts had complete but only momentary pleasure, not lasting object relations, as their basis. It was, rather, the brothers who, because of the sexual privation forced upon them by their jealous father, first experienced social life as we know it.

Prevented by the repressive father from achieving genital satisfaction with women, the brothers formed ties among themselves based on aim-inhibited libido, sometimes expressing itself in homosexual erotic ties among them. This aim-inhibited love became a part of what cemented them into an enduring group. But narcissism once again augments object love, through the process of identification. Forced to renounce his own narcissism, each young man clings to it in fantasy by creating the image of his own forfeited perfection as an "ego ideal" (a forerunner of the superego, which appeared first in *The Ego and the Id* [1923]). This in turn is based on the image of the full-fledged primal father he himself would like to be, preserved for him in cultural and phylogenetic memory. Unable to realize this idea, and seeing the futility of competing with his brothers for supremacy, he turns his sibling rivalry, by reaction formation, into a sense of equality and group solidarity, by the reasoning that "if one cannot be the favorite oneself, at all events nobody else shall be the favorite" (1921, 120).

He introjects as his ego ideal a leader who is, or at least can be mistaken for, a realization of what he aspires to. His fellows do likewise, and they thus share a common ego ideal, identifying with the leader by trying to mold their own egos to a likeness of the admired one.

The result is that they are all similar in having the same ego ideal and similar egos, and therefore they are able to identify with each other and thus love each other in a way closer to narcissism than to object love. Thus aim-inhibited self-love spilling over onto others seen as like oneself is the basis of long-lasting social ties. Since the primal horde no longer exists, the leaders who emerge are not true narcissistic primal fathers but simulacra of them who can overawe, fascinate, terrorize, and inspire love in a group. (Freud's prescience regarding fascism, then about to emerge, was uncanny.)

An implication of this analysis, not spelled out by Freud but with far-reaching implications for anthropology, is that social life among humans is structured around two axes: there is the axis of heterosexual coupling leading to biological reproduction; and there is the axis of society formed by aim-inhibited relations of identification based on libido which is neither hetero- nor homosexual, but which "shows a complete disregard for the aims of the genital organization of the libido" (1921, 141).

It follows of necessity then that the social ties of the "brother horde"—those which in fact constitute the more enduring "glue" of society—must be derived from pregenital erotic strivings, inhibited in aim and sublimated or transformed through reaction formation into cultural forms. These pregenital elements would include the oral and dependent, the anal and sadomasochistic, and the exhibitionistic and narcissistic components of human sexuality, which make their appearance earlier in childhood than genital ones.

Any society has to reconcile the claims and principles of both the genital and the pregenital axes of society. Thus, in some non-Western, nonliterate societies, the two strands are visibly separated; there is a men's society different from the realm of heterosexual reproduction. The two are linked by the fact that senior men are both married householders and fathers, and also high-ranking members of the male society. The ritual symbolism of such male societies is often replete with more or less transformed and sublimated pregenital erotic imagery.

By the time Freud wrote *Civilization and Its Discontents* in 1930, his theory had undergone still further revisions. He had introduced the tripartite Ego-Id-Superego structural model of the psyche in

The Ego and the Id (1923); and he had finally faced up to the implication of his late dual instinct theory, that aggression, pure and
simple, is an instinctual drive on an equal footing with the sexual
instinct. In 1930 Freud still sees culture and society arising out of
love and common work, to be sure; but this love is more and more
understood as derived from a primary narcissism that regards every other person as a potential enemy, rival, or inhibitor of one's
freedom; the aggression aroused in defense of this narcissism is
only by reaction formation turned into the highly ambivalent love
that characterizes society.

The first to thwart our boundless narcissism were our parents.
We internalize their prohibiting authority as the superego and
keep it energized by using our own aggression, now turned against
ourselves, to frighten ourselves into being "good" and renouncing
our Oedipal wishes in the interests of security and avoiding the
punishments of loss of love and of castration.

Now finally Freud has a grounding in his instinct theory for the
ambivalence of obsessional neurosis and of civilization: aim-
inhibited object love and narcissistic identification as group bonds
lie uneasily atop a repressed current of hatred and destructiveness,
the inhibition of which imposes the "obsessive" defenses upon society: the great interest in beauty, cleanliness, order, and love of one's
enemies so central to (Judeo-Christian) civilization's view of itself
betrays the fact that culture has to work overtime to inhibit and
defend against, by reaction formation, the violent anal sadistic
urges that arise when narcissism is infringed.

The source of the superego, for Freud, which acts as internal
guardian serving the interests of civilization rather than of our
own happiness, is, in the 1930 work, a blend of both our own inhibited and inturned aggression and the fact of a real external punishing authority. Again, our descent from the primal horde, and our
shared memory of the primal father and his murder, prepare us
(men) to respond to our own less than titanic fathers as substitutes
for them with the awe and terror the original father inspired by his
mere look.

With *Moses and Monotheism* (1939), Freud's final major book, the
journey is complete and the theory of culture can be viewed in its

fully evolved form. Readers have been distracted, in approaching this work, by numerous difficulties (not the least of which is the question of why Freud wrote it at all, in the period of Nazi ascendency). A close reading of the book will reveal, I believe, that neither the question of Moses's nationality, nor of whether there were two Moseses, nor whether Moses was a follower of Akhnaton, nor even whether Moses was killed in a revolt, is central to the argument. Rather, the book is a new exposition of the primal horde theory, this time explicitly set in the context of the history of Judeo-Christian civilization. Here for the first time the analogy between obsessional neurosis and Western religious history is systematically laid out.

The analogous pattern, repeated on the individual and collective level, is this sequence: "early trauma—defense—latency—outbreak of the neurosis—partial return of the repressed material" (1939, 80). The trauma is an overwhelming experience of a combined sexual, aggressive, and narcissistic nature. In the individual, it is the Oedipal fantasies; in society, the primal crime itself. The trauma gives rise to an active compulsion to repeat itself, and at the same time to an effort at defending against the impulse to repeat it. After remaining relatively dormant for a while, the conflict between impulse and defense reemerges under certain circumstances (such as, in individual psychology, in sleep or illness, when an instinct receives added strength, as the libido does at puberty, or when recent events remind one of the repressed material).

In a typical obsessional-compulsive neurosis, the initial trauma leaves a conflict between hostile wishes felt as deeds, and a fear of danger in the form of retaliatory castration. To ward off the danger, defenses are instituted, including reaction formation, whereby the hostile wish is converted into an elevated sense of justice and morality; isolation, through which thoughts and affects are kept apart and ideas left unconnected to avoid reexperiencing the whole fantasy; and undoing, in which the constantly asserted impulse needs to be counteracted with expiatory ritual. Latency is achieved in middle childhood with the installation of the superego and advancing cognitive abilities; but adolescence brings on new instinctual stresses leading to the outbreak of the repressed conflict in neurotic symptoms representing a compromise formation between the ambivalent wishes to express and to defend against the impulses.

If, for the sake of exposition, we accept the analogy between culture and the individual life, the comparable sequence in civilization would be this: first there is the primal murder, the trauma enacting aggression and motivated by sexual and narcissistic impulses. The compulsion to repeat the deed is warded off by the defenses established as the social prohibitions on incest and on killing the deified representative of the father; these renunciations are enforced by the shared memory of the slain patriarch, whose internalized authority empowers the cultural superego. After a period of development and latency, certain historical circumstances—the upheavals of the biblical era—bring about a remembrance of the primal crime. In response to the threatened return of the traumatic situation and the feared retaliation from the still-living memory of the jealous deity who visits the sins of the father upon the sons down through generations, actions and observances are undertaken which, as compromise formations, both express and defend against the hostile side of the ambivalent relations within society and toward the authority that maintains it. These observances become, first, the elaborate list of rules, prohibitions, and ritual observances of Judaism, and then the dramatic but ultimately failed attempt at liberation from them represented by Christianity. The latter, though ostensibly aiming at undoing the primal guilt through atoning sacrifice and thus making the code of laws unnecessary, instead deepens the guilt by recognizing that even rebellious wishes, as well as deeds, require punishment or hoped-for forgiveness.

I am quite convinced that Freud arrived at the construct of the primal crime not from reading Robertson Smith and Darwin, but by performing upon the central Christian ritual, the Eucharist or Mass, the same sort of analysis and reconstruction of early events he would have carried out had the same constellation of ideas and actions been presented to him as the fantasy or ceremony of an individual obsessional patient. The endlessly repeated sacrifice of an "innocent" son could only be a resolution of neurotic guilt concerning an original murder of (or death wish toward) a father by the guilty ringleader of a "band of brothers." In the communion ritual the innocence of the rebel is proclaimed at the same time as

His guilt is confessed by His execution; while the original wish for patricide is enacted insofar as the slain son is asserted to be identical with the deified father.

My assumption that the primal crime is a reconstruction from Christian ritual is supported by this quotation from Freud: "From the manner in which, in Christianity, this redemption is achieved— by the sacrificial death of a single person, who in this manner takes upon himself a guilt that is common to everyone—*we have been able to infer* what the first occasion may have been on which this primal guilt, which was also the beginning of civilization, was acquired" (1930, 136; my emphasis).

Freud himself recognized, of course, that the greatest difficulty in treating civilization as if it were an individual capable of having a neurosis is the question of how we are to suppose that contemporary people can be motivated, indeed compelled, by memories of events that occurred not in their own lives, but in ancient history. Though human actors, and not a hypostasized "civilization," are the subjects of Freud's drama his scheme requires them to act on knowledge they cannot be supposed to have gained by direct experience. How can this be?

In *Totem and Taboo*, contrary to widely held opinion, Freud does *not* suggest or even imply that the memory of the primal crime continues across generations by means of the "inheritance of acquired characteristics." While he does think that there must exist the inheritance of some psychical dispositions, he argues that those must be given "some sort of impetus in the life of the individual before they can be roused into actual operation" (1913, 158). And though he does not think that "direct communication and tradition" account for the transmission of the memories, he does *not* turn to genetic inheritance but rather to the encoding of unconscious ideas in *cultural symbolism*, a mode of information storage which, like genetic information but independent of it, is transmitted across generations. The relevant passage is worth quoting in full, since misunderstandings of this text are so commonplace:

[P]sychoanalysis has shown us that everyone possesses in his unconscious mental activity an apparatus which enables him to interpret other people's reactions, that is to undo the distortions which other people have imposed on the expression of their feelings. An unconscious understanding such as this of all the *customs, ceremonies, and dogmas* left behind by the original relation to the father may have made it possible for later generations to take over their heritage of emotion. (1913, 159; my emphasis).

In other words, everyone can perform unconsciously the analysis which Freud performs on, let us say, the Mass, and divine its real emotional message, which he or she then uses to give specific form to his or her own highly charged personal repressed fantasies—as I argued also that the audience does while watching *Oedipus Rex*.

As his career developed, Freud grew more and more convinced that symbolically disguised cultural inheritance in rites, symbols, and myths alone could not account for the strength of the Oedipal fantasies, and did come to insist that they were phylogenetically inherited. But to say that something is inherited phylogenetically is not—as all of biology attests—the same as saying that it requires the "inheritance of acquired characteristics." As Freud pointed out, a comparison with the case of animals shows that they too "have preserved memories of what was experienced by their ancestors" (1939, 100). That is to say, the beaver has a phylogenetic "memory" of how earlier beavers built dams; the migratory bird has a phylogenetic "memory" of the constellations of the night sky used as signals by its ancestors. The question of the mechanism by which this "memory" was acquired is the province of genetics and evolutionary theory, and by no means Freud's problem alone.

I thus conclude that it is quite possible to suppose that humans have a phylogenetic predisposition to construct fantasies and attach affects to them as if they were vitally real according to the scenario of the primal horde—whether or not such a state of affairs ever really existed, or whether the phylogenetically inherited constellation is any more strictly speaking a "memory," in the narrow sense, than is the bird's innate knowledge of the stars and how to respond to them literally a "memory" of something its first ancestor experienced. Whether the "events" symbolized in the Eucharist, for example, actually once occurred or not is a moot point; what is relevant is that each generation is capable of acting as if it understood the meaning of the ritual and were under the peremptory sway of the impulses and fears it enacts.

We can see, then, that Freud supposes that the "memories" and fantasies at the root of our civilization are carried along three channels: the personal, the cultural, and the phylogenetic. The individual has a memory, in the literal sense, of his or her own actual infantile Oedipal experience. This personal memory is formed against the backdrop of, and given shape to, on the one hand, by the species-specific human phylogenetic promptings that date back to our days as a social but precultural primate; and on the other by the culturally inherited symbolic forms—the "customs, ceremonies, and dogmas"—in which the particular traditions of the culture are encoded.

Personal memory can last only a lifetime, inscribed as it is in the tissue of a mortal organism. But civilization has continuity because memories, fantasies, myths, and ideas can travel across generations along two parallel tracks. One is genetic, and depends for its continuity on sexual reproduction; the other is cultural and involves the encoding of information in external vehicles—symbols in the broadest sense—the most highly charged of which draw energy from the libidinal, aggressive, and narcissistic impulses of childhood.

This "dual inheritance model" of cross-generational information transmission (Boyd and Richerson 1985; Paul 1987) accounts for the existence of the two axes of society to which I referred earlier: the heterosexual one is necessary to accomplish sexual (genetic) reproduction; while the "band of brothers" is bound by aim-inhibited nongenital libido turned to cultural sublimations. These two must cooperate (minimally) to reproduce the totality of human society, but there is an inherent tension between them. As Freud says, "civilization behaves toward sexuality as a people or stratum of its population does which has subjected another one to its exploitation. Fear of a revolt by the suppressed elements drives it to stricter precautionary measures" (1930, 107).

If, as I think we must, we reject the literal historicity of the primal crime, as well as the idea of the history of civilization being like maturation from infancy on through stages comparable to those in an individual life, then we cannot accept at face value

Freud's analogy between Judeo-Christian religion and obsessional neurosis. But I propose that our rejection of these aspects of Freud's cultural thought should not lead us to ignore the fact that the parallels he cites are highly persuasive, indicating that the fantasies, impulses, defenses, and symbolism observed clinically in obsessional personalities—and culturally in the rites, symbols, and traditions of our civilization—are closely related if not identical. The difference between them would remain that in religious institutions the instinctual conflict and its outcome is turned to the constructive function of uniting a group of surly individuals into an enduring society knit together by the strongest of instinctual emotions, namely libido, aggression, and narcissism. In the neurosis the same work is done to nobody's benefit.

If we accept that the individual memory of the childhood nuclear fantasy and its outcome is prepared for and augmented by the influence of *both* phylogenetic predispositions—the nature and extent of which has yet to be determined by research—*and* cultural tradition embodied in inherited symbolic forms and practices; and if we accept, furthermore, the implication of Freud's cultural works that there are two different social axes representing the two different modes of transmission of information across generations—the genetic, sexual one, and the cultural one based on aim-inhibited nonreproductive libido; then we also arrive at sound theoretical support for the tripartite model of the psyche. The agency of the organism proper (the ego) negotiates its way through reality, always prompted by the (often conflicting) imperatives of the sexual, directly instinctual, phylogenetic "program" (the id); and the asexual, nongenital, cultural program (the superego). Individuals, as well as societies and cultures they form, must take the needs of all of those into account in any effective compromise. Investigating the ways they do this (or fail to do so) is the project for a systematic comparative ethnography yet to be undertaken.

References

Boyd, R., and Richerson, P. 1985. *Culture and the Evolutionary Process.* Chicago: University of Chicago Press.

Darwin, C. 1871. *The Descent of Man*, 2 vols. London: John Murray.

Durkheim, Emile. 1912. *Les formes elémentaires de la vie religieuse: Le système totémique en Australie*. Paris: F. Alcan.

Ferenczi, S. 1913. Ein kleiner Hahnemann. *Int. Zeitschrift für Psychoanalyse* 1:240–246.

Frazer, J. G. 1910. *Totem and Exogamy*. London: Macmillan and Co.

Freud, S. 1900. The interpretation of dreams. *S.E.* 4 and 5.

———. 1901. The psychopathology of everyday life. *S.E.* 6.

———. 1905. Jokes and their relation to the unconscious. *S.E.* 8.

———. 1907. Obsessive actions and religious practices. *S.E.* 9:115–128.

———. 1909a. Analysis of a phobia in a five-year-old boy. *S.E.* 10:1–147.

———. 1909b. Notes upon a case of obsessional neurosis. *S.E.* 10:151–250.

———. 1910. Leonardo Da Vinci and a memory of his childhood. *S.E.* 11:59–138.

———. 1913. Totem and taboo. *S.E.* 13:1–161.

———. 1914. On narcissism: An introduction. *S.E.* 14: 67–140.

———. 1918. From the history of an infantile neurosis. *S.E.* 17:1–122.

———. 1920. Beyond the pleasure principle. *S.E.* 18:1–64.

———. 1921. Group psychology and the analysis of the ego. *S.E.* 18:65–144.

———. 1923. The ego and the id. *S.E.* 19:1–59.

———. 1926. Inhibitions, symptoms and anxiety. *S.E.* 20:75–176.

———. 1928. Dostoevsy and parricide. *S.E.* 21:173–194.

———. 1930. Civilization and its discontents. *S.E.* 21:57–146.

———. 1939. Moses and monotheism: Three essays. *S.E.* 23:1–138.

Freud, S., and Oppenheim, E. 1911. Dreams in folklore. *S.E.* 12:175–203.

Geertz, C. 1973. *The Interpretation of Cultures*. New York: Basic Books.

Paul, R. A. 1976. Did the primal crime take place? *Ethos* 4:311–352.

———. 1982. *The Tibetan Symbolic World: Psychoanalytic Explorations*. Chicago: University of Chicago Press.

———. 1987. The individual and society in biological and cultural anthropology. *Cultural Anthropology* 2:80–93.

Robertson Smith, W. 1894. *Lectures on the Religion of the Semites*. London: A. and C. Black.

2

Culture and Neurosis: A Discussion of Dr. Paul's Presentation on Freud's Anthropology

Thomas S. Wolman

In his excellent discussion of Freud's cultural writings, Robert A. Paul asks, "How can the insights into individual psychology gained through the techniques of psychoanalysis illuminate the cultural, collective life of people in society?" In my response to Paul's paper, I take up the reverse question of how Freud's mass psychology can enrich our understanding of the individual psyche. Paul notes that "Freud's individual psychology itself was never the isolated, hermetically sealed internal system sometimes caricatured by its detractors." Neither was Freud's mass psychology a simple "summation" of the psychology of individuals. His cultural writings cannot be reduced to mere exercises in applied psychoanalysis. They are just as much "about" psychoanalysis as the *Interpretation of Dreams*, or the *Psychopathology of Everyday Life*. I therefore assume that they are addressed to me as an analyst, in addition to other audiences, and that they have something to say about the problems facing psychoanalysis as a collectivity. In my discussion,

I want to enlarge upon just one small corner of this very wide field surveyed by Dr. Paul.

Freud (1907) recognized the profound kinship between psyche and culture in his famous aphorism comparing an obsessional neurosis to an "individual religiosity," and religion to a "universal obsessional neurosis." He observed that religious ceremonials are subject to the same distortions as neurotic symptoms, raising the question whether "some civilizations, or some epochs of civilization— possibly the whole of mankind—have become neurotic" (1930, 144). According to historians such as J. Huizinga (1954), such a generalization might apply to the culture of the high Middle Ages, when the collective religious life reached such a peak of intensity that it rendered individual neurosis unnecessary.

Freud (1930) argues that advancing civilization tends to encroach upon individual sexual life by requiring "that there shall be a single kind of sexual life for everyone." By disregarding "the dissimilarities, whether innate or acquired, in the sexual constitution of human beings," it "cuts off a fair number of them from sexual enjoyment, and so becomes the source of serious injustice" (p. 104). Indeed, in Freud's judgment, the sexual life of civilized people is so severely impaired that "it sometimes gives the impression of being in process of involution as a function, just as our teeth and hair seem to be as organs" (p. 105). The resulting loss of happiness gives rise to a collective sense of guilt—the "symptom" par excellence of the "universal neurosis." In *Civilization and Its Discontents* (1930) Freud speculates boldly that "the sense of guilt produced by civilization is not perceived as such either, and remains to a large extent unconscious, or appears as a sort of malaise, a dissatisfaction, for which people seek other motivations" (p. 135).

In contemporary nonindustrial societies that do not distinguish between psyche and culture, the Oedipus complex, and one might even say neurosis, appears as a purely collective phenomenon. The laws and marriage rules of such societies are the "cultural equivalents of the prohibition on incest" (p. 7). And "the institution of society thus rests on the measures taken to suppress the wishes of the Oedipus complex" (p. 10). According to anthropologists such as Lévi-Strauss, the efficacy of this "structural Oedipus complex" "derives from the fact that it brings into play a proscriptive agency (the prohibition against incest) which bars the way to naturally sought satisfaction and forms an indissoluble link between wish and law" (Laplanche and Pontalis 1973, 286).

Even in modern society, the dichotomy between psyche and culture is never absolute for Freud. "The greater individual variability of (neurotic) ceremonial actions in contrast to the stereotyped character of rituals" (1907, 119) is strictly relative. Even the private nature of neurosis, "as opposed to the public and communal character of religious observances" (p. 119) is subject to qualifications and exceptions. Freud himself denies any difference on the grounds that "while the minutiae of religious ceremonial are full of significance and have a symbolic meaning, those of neurotics seem foolish and senseless" (p. 119). The only thing, he writes, that distinguishes a neurotic ceremonial from a daily ritual is "the special conscientiousness with which it is carried out and the anxiety which follows upon its neglect" (p. 118). Indeed, the ubiquitous rituals of daily life are neither full-fledged religious rites nor neurotic symptoms, residing instead in the "no-man's land" of vestigial religious culture or the psychopathology of everyday life, depending on the point of view.

One might say that in modern society the psyche tends to feed on the host culture like a parasite. It would always much rather exploit an already existing structure than have to construct one from scratch. Thus it will prefer an existing religious ceremonial to the work of creating a new neurotic symptom. Freud (1930) writes, in this regard, that "the benefits of order are incontestable. It enables men to use space and time to the best advantages, while conserving their psychical forces" (p. 93). He also notes (1913) that "there is an intellectual function in us which demands unity, connection and intelligibility from any material, whether of perception or thought, that comes within its grasp" (p. 95). To this end, the host culture provides a whole system of meaningful references, props, and buttresses that hold the psyche in place.

The ordering of society is largely a function of law. Freud (1930) defines the rule of law as "a kind of compulsion to repeat which, when a regulation has been laid down once and for all, decides when, where and how a thing shall be done" (p. 93). This law allies itself with the psyche's repressive forces to limit the freedom of the individual. Thus "civilization is built up upon a renunciation of instinct" (1907, 125). It "obtains mastery over the individual's dangerous desire for aggression by weakening and disarming it and by setting up an agency within him to watch over it, a garrison in a conquered city" (1930, 124). Freud draws a distinction between this "cultural superego," whose "actual demands often remain unconscious in the background," and the individual's noisy self-reproaches. "If we bring them (the demands) to conscious knowledge," writes Freud, "we find that they coincide with the precepts of the prevailing cultural super-ego" (p. 142).

And just as the law provides the legal framework for the superego, other cultural resources can offer the techniques for self-cure. Freud concedes (1930) that culture can be therapeutic when it provides "powerful deflections, which cause us to make light of our misery; substitutive satisfactions, which diminish it; and intoxicating substances, which make us insensitive to it" (p. 75). Of all these methods, Freud accorded the most value to activities that function as sublimatory channels. Of these, the domain of work occupies a privileged position: "No other technique for the conduct of life attaches the individual so firmly to reality as laying emphasis on work; for his work at least gives him a secure place in a portion of reality, in the human community" (p. 80).

"One gains the most," Freud writes, "if one can sufficiently heighten the yield of pleasure from the sources of psychical and intellectual work. When this is so, fate can do little against one. A satisfaction of this kind, such as the artist's joy in creating, in giving his phantasies body, or a scientist's in solving problems or discovering truths, has a special quality" (p. 79).

Civilization also supplies the means, according to Freud (1930), of a young person's "detaching himself from his family . . . by means of puberty and initiation rites" (p. 103). In his classic study of the Bar Mitzvah rite, Jacob Arlow (1951) shows how a religious rite can actually help to master the conflicts surrounding the Oedipus complex. The potential therapeutic effects of the rite include partial resolution of father-son ambivalence, transition to sexual maturity, relief of guilt over masturbation, initiation of detachment from the father, mastery of guilt and inferiority over sibling rivalry, consolidation of superego, new sublimatory channels, and further separation of the boy from his mother.

Arlow notes, however, that the effects of the Bar Mitzvah rite are far from uniform. In some individuals, the rite helps to precipitate a transitory obsessional neurosis. Arlow seems to imply that the Bar Mitzvah acts like a moderately potent drug, which still pales in comparison to primitive initiation rites. He contrasts the continued vitality of the ceremony to that of other rites, such as examinations, which exist only in vestigial form (Flugel 1939), and he remarks on the heavy demand for this rite, even amoung the nonobservant. At several points he notes the close association between the Bar Mitzvah and other rites, such as a birth, wedding, or graduation ritual. Although not stated in so many words, one might conclude that the therapeutic effect of the ceremony derives from multiple displacements, in the manner of a multiply determined symptom.

In another important cultural study, Aries (1974) has outlined the antitherapeutic effect of the absence of a rite—the death ritual. He writes that "death in the hospital is no longer the occasion of a ritual ceremony, over which the dying person presides amidst his assembled relatives and friends. Death is a technical phenomenon obtained by a cessation of care, a cessation determined in a more or less avowed way by a decision of the doctor and the hospital team" (p. 88). The burden of dealing with death now falls on the individual who "only has the right to cry if no one else can see or hear. Solitary and shameful mourning is the only recourse, like a sort of masturbation" (p. 90). Aries concludes that "the choking back of sorrow, the forbidding of its public manifestation, and the obligation to suffer alone and secretly, has aggravated the trauma stemming from the loss of a dear one" (p. 92).

One of my patients used to complain bitterly of the absence of appropriate ceremonies for dealing with loss. She used to note ruefully that society has no resources to help with the private, intangible losses, like the loss of an ideal, a friendship, or an unborn child. This patient depended heavily on the ready-made channels in social, occupational, political, and religious life to support her shaky sense of identity and precarious inner life. One could say that her heavy dependency on civilization's ordering function spared her from an obsessional neurosis. However, she paid dearly for the relative paucity of traditional culture in modern society.

It would seem that culture is just as susceptible to the fate of "involution" as that of individual sexuality. Under these conditions, the psyche is thrown back more and more upon its own resources. The decline of religion has necessitated the return of "individual religiosities." Neurosis may be viewed as an attempt to compensate for the gaps and rents in civilization. The symptoms of the obsessional neurotic may indeed seem like a caricature of religion, as Freud suggests (1907), but might they not also contain an element of homage? Aries (1974) writes that our failure to collectively symbolize death brings about a return of the repressed in the form of "sadistic literature and in violent death in our daily life" (p. 93). Indeed, extreme fragmentation of culture favors the existence of nonneurotic solutions that threaten the very integrity of the psyche.

The experience of the Great War helped to disabuse Freud of many of his own illusions about Western civilization. He interpreted the widespread disillusion as the inevitable result of the sudden destruction of cherished illusions. These illusions tended to hide the hypocrisy upon which much of so-called civilization is based. He wrote: "It is undeniable that our contemporary civilization favours the production of this form of hypocrisy to an extraordinary extent. One might venture to say that it is built upon such hypocrisy, and that it would have to submit to far-reaching modifications if people were to undertake to live in accordance with psychological truth" (1915, 284). The state of illusion is analogous to the secondary revision which gives to dreams the appearance of intelligibility, coherence, and completeness. But like dreams, it requires but a small dose of reality for the whole structure to unravel like a house of cards. Civilization "creates no impenetrable armour against the arrows of fortune," he cautions, "and it habitually fails when the source of suffering is a person's own body" (1930, 80). Not surprisingly he questioned whether it is realistic to expect civilization to contain the destructive forces that lie dormant in the human mind. "Civilization has to use its utmost efforts," he writes, "in order to set limits to man's aggressive instincts and to hold the manifestations of them in check by psychical reaction-formations" (p. 112).

Indeed, it was precisely at a time when science appeared capable of solving the problems of civilization that psychoanalysis appeared in history. Although it borrowed the trappings of medicine, psychoanalysis was soon recognized as a new cultural phenomenon in its own right. Almost from the beginning, it sought to reclaim the lost treasures of the old culture, in the inner life of the unconscious mind. One way it accomplished this was by patiently reconstructing the psychical equivalents of the ancient rites. Thus it provided a new setting for the work of mourning, and for the labor of giving birth to the self. Arlow (1951) mentions a patient who "sought in the analysis what he felt Bar Mitzvah might have given him—permission to repudiate the authority of the father, assurance of being accepted as an equal" (p. 370). Analysis has itself become a kind of all-purpose rite of passage, standing in for a marriage, birth, funeral, or graduation, depending on circumstances.

Since its birth, psychoanalysis has spawned a whole new therapeutic culture that has incorporated many of its techniques and insights. This subculture now performs the therapeutic function that analysis held at its origin, and in the process has co-opted its original pool of neurotic patients. Moreover, it has tried to assimilate analysis into itself by creating incentives for analysts to exaggerate their curative potential, and by blurring the distinction between analysis and other therapies. In effect psychoanalysis has found itself simultaneously pushed toward the cultural margins in the "widening scope of psychoanalysis," and pulled into the cultural mainstream.

These developments call analysis into question and force it to reexamine its relationship to its host culture. Is analysis in danger of becoming another species of cultural indoctrination? Or does it merely borrow the trappings of therapeusis in order to do something else? Does this relationship vary from one host culture to another? Has analysis remained on the margin of culture—that is, as the analyzer of the "borderline"—or is it now part of the cultural mainstream?

An essential question is whether there exists a psychoanalytic function that exists in common between analysis (in the pure culture) and the host culture. Arlow seems to imply that a cultural rite may play this role if it stimulates conflict rather than tranquilizes it and challanges the individual to go through a process of psychical work. Paul also seems to accept this idea when he quotes Freud to the effect that

Psychoanalysis has shown us that everyone possesses in his unconscious mental activity an apparatus which enables him to interpret other people's reactions, that is to undo the distortions which other people have imposed on the expression of their feelings. An unconscious understanding such as this of all the customs, ceremonies, and dogmas left behind by the original relation to the father may have made it possible for later generations to take over their heritage of emotion. (1913, 159)

I wonder if Freud's speculations on the discontents of civilization apply equally well to analysis. It is interesting that Freud's pessimism in *Civilization and Its Discontents* goes hand in hand with his pessimism over the results of analysis. Yet he never meant to minimize the benefits of either one. The aim of analysis was only to convert neurosis into ordinary human unhappiness. But if the host culture values the pursuit of happiness, then the fate of analysis may be to become the repository of that chronic malaise that is the condition of civilized man.

References

Aries, P. 1974. *Western Attitudes toward Death: From the Middle Ages to the Present.* Baltimore, Md: Johns Hopkins University Press.

Arlow, J. 1951. A psychoanalytic study of a religious initiation rite: Bar Mitzvah. *Psychoanalytic Study of the Child* 6:353–374.

Flugel, J. C. 1939. The examination as initiation rite and anxiety situation. *Int. J. Psycho-Analysis* 20.

Freud, S. 1907. Obsessive actions and religious practices. *S.E.* 9:115–128.

———. 1913. Totem and taboo. *S.E.* 13:1–161.

———. 1915. Thoughts for the times on war and death. *S.E.* 14:273–301.

———. 1930. Civilization and its discontents. *S.E.* 21:59–145.

Huizinga, J. 1954. *The Waning of the Middle Ages.* Garden City, N.Y.: Doubleday Anchor Books.

Laplanche, J., and Pontalis, J.-B. 1973. *The Language of Psycho-Analysis.* New York: W. W. Norton.

3

Freud at Meynert's Clinic: The Paradoxical Influence of Psychiatry on the Development of Psychoanalysis

Albrecht Hirschmüller

The relationship between psychoanalysis and psychiatry has been strained for decades. In Germany there has been a strong preference for a biological approach, and psychoanalytic theory seems to be of diminishing importance for university psychiatry. When in 1905 Eugen Bleuler, the noted Swiss psychiatrist, published an essay on "Freudian mechanisms in the symptomatology of psychoses," Freud wrote him a postcard with the hopeful sentence: "I am sure, we shall soon have conquered psychiatry."[1] In 1925 Freud could speak of a sort of *pénétration pacifique* of psychoanalytic viewpoints in German psychiatry.[2] On the other hand, he never lost his doubts that psychoanalytic therapy would ever really be able to help psychotic patients, thereby opposing the views of his pupils Paul Federn, Paul Schilder, Robert Waelder, Ludwig Binswanger, and others. In 1928, in a letter to the Hungarian psychiatrist István Hollós, the seventy-three-year-old Freud admits a lack of love for severely disturbed psychiatric patients, his anger with them, and his feeling that they were alien to him and to everything human.

He called this feeling "a peculiar kind of intolerance which un-doubtedly disqualifies me as a psychiatrist."[3] I agree with Dr. Eis-sler that this letter shows Freud in all his human greatness.[4]

Why does Freud mention his attitude toward such patients? In his private practice he did not see many of them—we know of only a few psychotic patients with whom he dealt. If we want to recon-struct his experiences with clinical psychiatry, we must go back to his postgraduate medical education, when he worked at Vienna's Psychiatric University Hospital from May to September 1883. It seems to me that some switch must have been pulled during those months that set the future paths of psychiatry and psychoanalysis on a predominantly divergent course.

What sort of psychiatry did he become acquainted with? Who were the people and what were the institutions like in which he worked? Was psychiatry at that time really such a fruitless branch of science, as Jones has stated? How does this square with the fact that Theodor Meynert, Freud's chief, was regarded as one of the leading figures of psychiatry in Europe, a man who had been offered the psychiatric chair and directorship of the Burghölzli in Zürich several years before? Was Meynert not trying to base psychiatry on the firm grounds of neuroanatomy, the very field in which the young Freud had had his scientific beginnings? Would it not have been a natural consequence for Freud to follow in the footsteps of Meynert?

Thirty years ago, the Gicklhorns answered this question by claiming that Freud simply had not been willing to compromise;[5] had he done so, like his colleague Wagner-Jauregg, he certainly would have had a successful career. Dr. Eissler promptly and vigor-ously refuted this tendentious argument.[6] But the question why Freud did not follow in Meynert's footsteps remains unanswered. In my habilitation thesis I investigated as precisely as possible the background, the personal and scientific milieu, and Freud's spe-cific experiences while working at Meynert's clinic.[7]

I will begin with a few words about the general situation of psychiatry and neurology in Europe in those years, and then dis-cuss the specific situation in Vienna. Next, I will deal with the patients Freud encountered, and finally I will discuss his personal situation during those months.

Psychiatry and Neurology in the 1880s

What was the state of psychiatry and neurology in the German-speaking countries of the 1880s? The reigning paradigm, derived from Wilhelm Griesinger, was that mental diseases were diseases of the brain, and the other tendency of Griesinger's psychiatry, namely his psychological argumentation, had been quickly and thoroughly forgotten. Experimental psychology was in its infancy: Wilhelm Wundt's laboratory in Leipzig had been founded in 1879, with Ernst Kraepelin as its first medical doctor. In later years, Kraepelin would fight for the rightful role of physiological psychology in psychiatry. Within the psychiatry of the 1880s the main conflict was between what Karl Jaspers called *Universitätspsychiatrie* and *Anstaltspsychiatrie*, or university psychiatry and asylum psychiatry, respectively.[8] Generations of psychiatrists had done their best to care for the insane, examining and classifying their forms of illness and fighting for their rights. Now pathological anatomy and histology were said to be the decisive methods in investigating those diseases, and psychiatry was considered nothing more than another branch of the neurosciences. Consequently, neuropsychiatrists claimed competence to treat all mental and nervous diseases, although the latter had previously belonged to the field of internal medicine. After the rapid developments in anatomy, physiology, and pathology of the nervous system in the second half of the nineteenth century, the process of specialization found its logical culmination in the foundation of the German Neurological Society in 1907.

In order to see more clearly the main scientific discussions of the early 1880s I examined four German psychiatric periodicals from the years 1882, 1883, and 1884 (table 3.1). Among 1,436 articles and reviews, 347, that is, 25 percent, dealt with organic neurology, Berlin being the center for this type of work; 56 (4 percent) with neuropsychiatry, mostly emanating from Vienna; 283 (20 percent) with theoretical psychiatry; and 382 (27 percent) with practical psychiatry. In the field of organic neurology, attention was focused on the question of epilepsy and on the relationship between syphilis and general paralysis of the insane. Interest in hysteria and

Table 3.1
Psychiatric Periodicals, 1882–1884

1. *Allgemeine Zeitschrift für Psychiatrie*
2. *Archiv für Psychiatrie und Nervenkrankheiten*
3. *Zentralblatt für Nervenheilkunde*
4. *Jahrbücher für Psychiatrie* (Vienna)

Subject	Number	%	Orig.	%	Rev.	%
Theoretical psychiatry	283	19.71	50	15.82	233	20.80
Practical psychiatry	382	26.60	62	19.62	320	28.57
Neuro-psychiatry	56	3.90	24	7.59	32	2.86
Neuro-anatomy	30	2.09	20	6.33	10	0.89
Organic neurology	347	24.16	107	33.86	240	21.43
Functional nervous diseases	71	4.94	12	3.80	59	5.27
Forensic psychiatry	230	16.02	33	10.44	197	17.59
Experimental psychology	37	2.58	8	2.53	29	2.59
Total	1,436	100.00	316	100.00	1,120	100.00

hypnosis, especially within the context of the work of Charcot in Paris, was growing slowly.

If we look at the biographies of the doctors of Freud's generation who were equally interested in nervous diseases, we get the impression that it was considerably difficult at that time to find a position allowing them to earn a living while pursuing their scientific interests. If they chose to work in internal medicine (like Strümpell), nervous diseases could only be a small part of their activities. If they worked in a psychiatric institution (like Wagner-Jauregg), they had to deal mainly with psychotic patients and had to face enormous practical problems providing psychiatric treatment with insufficient means. Some doctors (like Möbius) tried to find places at outpatient clinics for nervous diseases, but this often failed, and then their only recourse was to settle down as general practitioners and restrict scientific work in brain anatomy and neurophysiology to the evening hours. That is what happened to Ludwig Edinger and to Constantin von Monakow, two of the most gifted brain researchers, who attained their university positions only after many years of great personal sacrifice.

Meynert and Psychiatry in Vienna

Let us now turn to a description of the psychiatric institutions in Vienna. First, there was the Psychiatric Asylum of Lower Austria; it was founded in 1856, had 700 beds and was located just outside the city limits. A part of this asylum fulfilled the function of a university hospital; it was called the First Psychiatric Clinic and was under the direction of Max Leidesdorf. Second, there was a psychiatric section in the General Hospital of Vienna, with 110 beds, under the direction of Theodor Meynert; part of it was called the Second Psychiatric Clinic of the University of Vienna. This is the section I call "Meynert's clinic." Following an old tradition, this clinic was obliged to accept and observe any patient who became mentally ill in Vienna or its surroundings. In 1883 the clinic admitted no fewer than 1,655 patients, more than 5 each day, Monday to Friday. The wards were permanently overcrowded, so the doctors' first interest was to transfer patients into other institutions as quickly as possible, with the exception of those patients who seemed to be of some scientific interest. On the average, patients remained in Meynert's clinic no longer than eleven days. If further hospitalization was deemed necessary, those who were natives of Vienna were transferred to the already-mentioned Asylum of Lower Austria. If they were born in another part of the huge Austro-Hungarian empire, they would be transferred to other asylums, some of them several hundred miles away, though it was first necessary to obtain permission of the local government. Patients remained in these asylums more than eighteen months on average, a figure that clearly shows the fundamental difference with the situation at Meynert's clinic.

Five doctors, including Meynert, cared for the patients, handled their admission and release, wrote case reports, and so on. Personal contacts between doctors and patients were mostly limited to visitations in the large bedrooms every morning and afternoon. The plans of the wards do not show any room dedicated to private consultation between doctor and patient. It is self-evident that under such circumstances only a superficial contact between doctors and patients was possible.

Let us now turn to the life and work of Theodor Meynert. Meynert was born in Dresden, Saxony, in 1833, but lived in Vienna with his family since the age of seven. His father was a writer and journalist, his mother an opera singer. She is said to have been a beautiful but cool person. We know nearly nothing about Meynert's childhood. During his university studies he seems to have lived a difficult, erratic life. This phase came to an end when he married in 1861. His wife Johanna was an intelligent, warm-hearted, energetic woman. She was deeply influential in helping Meynert achieve a period of calm and fruitful creativity. The couple had three children. After having passed his medical examinations, Meynert worked as an assistant doctor and began to study brain anatomy. With the support of the noted pathologist Rokitansky, he became *Privatdozent* in 1864; after he worked as a prosector (doctor in charge of autopsies) at the Asylum of Lower Austria for a few years, his *venia legendi* was extended to "psychiatry based upon structure and function of the nervous system."[9] In 1870 he became the first professor of psychiatry in Vienna and head of the psychiatric clinic. This decision was violently criticized because of his lack of experience in clinical psychiatry: he had worked in psychiatric wards only for a few months.

After 1875 Meynert was at the peak of his career. Young doctors from everywhere came to listen to his lectures and to work in his laboratory, and he moved among the upper class of the bourgeoisie in Vienna. Unfortunately, the rest of his life was shadowed by a series of severe personal losses, beginning with the death of his mentor Rokitansky in 1878, followed by the death of his wife in 1879. After this event he wrote in a letter that he felt like a frog whose forebrain had been cut away and who could only jump when hit, but not perform any spontaneous movement.[10] One year later, his sister, who had been caring for his children, died, followed by his mother at the end of 1882. His second wife, whom he married in 1882, was never able to replace Johanna. She was burdened with caring for the three children and for Meynert's father and Johanna's mother, all of whom lived in the same house. She soon became pregnant and gave birth to a daughter in July 1883. Precisely during the months that Freud spent at the clinic, Meynert was deeply involved in this complicated family situation, and he was often absent. One year later Meynert's situation became even worse when his beloved and very gifted sixteen-year-old son died of the measles. Meynert never recovered from his deep depression. In

1892 his youngest daughter, then eight years old, died, and his own death came only a few months later. These heavy blows may shed some light on the bitterness, rigidity, and sarcasm attributed to Meynert, and on the many quarrels and polemics he fought.

I have already mentioned the fundamental orientation of Meynert's psychiatric system. Indeed he contributed much to our knowledge of brain anatomy. He discovered motor and sensory tracts in the brain stem and the connections to the cerebellum. He was the first to describe the histological structure of the brain cortex. But his attempt to found clinical psychiatry on the basis of neuroanatomy failed. It is certainly not by chance that his textbook on psychiatry[11] remained fragmentary. The first volume, which appeared in 1884, contains chapters on anatomy and physiology of the forebrain and a few pages on clinical psychiatry. It ends, strangely enough, in the middle of a sentence. The second volume never appeared.

The main problem of Meynert's system can be shown with a small example. As early as 1864 he published a case history of a woman who suffered from coordinative disorders.[12] The autopsy disclosed atrophy of the cerebellum and the pons. I am quite sure that today we would conclude that this woman suffered from a neurodegenerative disorder. Meynert, however, found it significant that she had fallen ill after a sudden shock and indulged in far-fetched speculations about the influence of psychic phenomena on blood circulation and brain structures. Similar mechanistic ideas can be found in quite a few of his publications. We should be aware that his contemporaries did not criticize him for his organistic approach, but for his neoromantic, speculative way of thinking. His style of speech and writing was fascinating but often unclear and overloaded with metaphors. This tendency became even more pronounced in his later works. When Barney Sachs, the American neurologist, translated Meynert's lectures into English, he earned deep admiration from Edinger, who had not found these lectures understandable even in German.

Freud had listened to Meynert's lectures when he was a student and was very much impressed by them. But when he began to work at Meynert's clinic, having undergone the strict education of Brücke's physiology, he must have become quickly aware that Meynert's approach of dealing only with brain-structure and brain-nourishment would not really help him understand the psychopathological mechanisms of his insane patients.

The Patients at Meynert's Service

What can we say about the patients at Meynert's clinic? The published annual reports do not draw a distinct picture of them. A couple of years ago I began to search for the original case histories. In Vienna I was told that no such case reports from Meynert's clinic had been preserved. In the archives of the former Asylum of Lower Austria I found nine case reports in Freud's handwriting. These patients, all of them women, had been transferred from Meynert's clinic. Thirty-three original case histories from the male division of Meynert's clinic, all in Freud's handwriting, are in the possession of the Sigmund Freud Archives in Washington, D.C. They had been acquired from an antiquarian many years ago. Through the courtesy of Dr. Eissler I received copies of this material. Four more case histories from the same period but including handwritten records of other doctors were found in Freud's home at Maresfield Gardens, London, and transferred to the Freud archives in 1988. It was Dr. Blum who kindly allowed me to make use of them. Finally, a bundle of case histories was unearthed in the late 1960s in Vienna by the novelist Irving Stone while he was researching his Freud novel.[13] He made photocopies of them and had them translated "from medical German into normal German and from there into English," as he said. Typewritten copies of both—the German and the English version— were prepared. In the meantime, the originals in Vienna have disappeared. When I asked Mr. Stone for his photocopies, he was sorry to say he could not find them. But copies of his transcriptions had been sent to the Chicago Institute for Psychoanalysis, where Ernest S. Wolf wrote an article about them in 1973.[14] Through the courtesy of both Mr. Stone and Dr. Wolf I finally received copies of this material. It consists of forty-eight case histories from the Asylum of Lower Austria, dating from the years 1880 to 1885. Forty-three of them had been transferred there from Meynert's clinic. Only three cases show Freud's name. The original German text was reconstructed as carefully as possible. As a result we now have ninety-two case histories, half of them written by Freud, half of them by other doctors.

I shall now try to give a brief idea of what those case reports are like. If one looks at the case histories and the terminology used, what is really meant is often unclear, especially when there may not be a corresponding word in English. I present a list with the diagnoses of the case histories in alphabetical order and in the original German text for those who are familiar with the German language. The diagnoses are very heterogeneous: some are in German, others in Latin, some remain on the level of symptomatology, others contain hypotheses about etiology, and so on (see table 3.2). If we try to summarize these diagnoses into the categories of our time, we might arrive at the diagram shown in table 3.3. I need not say how problematic it is to project modern diagnostic terms into the past.

Twelve percent of the patients were assumed to have alcohol problems. On 5 May, a fifty-five-year old shoemaker[15] came to Meynert's clinic diagnosed as having "Säuferwahnsinn, delirium potatorum." He suffered from delusions and optical and acoustical hallucinations, tremors of the hands and the tongue, and an enlarged liver. After ten days he was discharged as "cured." He seems to have suffered from a mild form of delirium tremens.

A second group of patients suffered from a disease that was very common then but is rather rare today: a thirty-four-year old textile worker[16] was in a euphoric state, displaying megalomania and lacking a sense of reality. Freud ascertained that the patient did not know the date or address where he lived and made errors in simple calculations. The somatic state showed the pupils to be without any light reaction, the left one wider, the reflexes not to be found. No doubt this patient suffered from a typical general paresis. Freud quickly diagnosed this disease. One month later he notes that no change had occurred and that the patient was being transferred to an asylum near his hometown in Bohemia.

Other forms of illness seem more familiar to psychiatrists of our era. Table 3.4 shows an example of the first group of case reports I mentioned, written on a special form for patients to be transferred to an asylum. It is the first of a four-page form with a long list of very detailed questions about the patient. Freud, however, did not answer all forty-two questions on it. The twenty-one-year-old patient, Margarethe P.,[17] a nun, daughter of a professor, had the idea that a priest was the devil, and she had hallucinated sexual inter-

Table 3.2
Diagnoses at Meynert's Clinic—Original Terms (in numbers of cases)

Alkoholismus	3
Alkoholismus chronicus	2
Anoia	2
Anoia ex Alkoholismo	1
Anoia (Status epilepticus)	1
Aufregung u. Wahnideen	1
Aufsteigende Paralyse	1
Blödsinn	3
Chronischer Alkoholismus	1
Chronischer Wahnsinn	6
Encephalitis	1
Epilepsie mit Geistesstörung, Blödsinn als Folge von chronischem Alkoholismus und epileptischen Anfällen	1
Epilepsie mit Geistesstörung; Blödsinn mit Wahnsinn	1
Epilepsie; Blödsinn	1
Epileptischer Blödsinn	1
Halluzinationen und Erregung	1
Halluzinatorische Verworrenheit	2
In observatione	1
Lyssa	1
Mania	1
Manie mit Lähmung; Blödsinn mit progressiver Paralyse; nach Schlaganfall	1
Manie; Delirium tremens	2
Manie; Dipsomanie	1
Melancholie	2
Meningitis	1
Observatio (Alkoholismus)	1
Originäre Verrücktheit	1
Paralysis traumatica	1
Paralytische Geistesstörung	2
Paranoia chronica	1
Progressive Paralyse	6

course with him. When she was admitted, she was highly excited; six weeks later, after she had calmed down a bit, she was discharged. But she soon had to be rehospitalized. "Ganz unzugänglich," "totally unapproachable," wrote Freud. The most important questions are to be found at the end of the form: Is the patient

Table 3.3
Diagnoses at Meynert's Clinic—Modern
Categories (in percentages)

Delirium tremens and chronic alcoholism	12
General paresis	18
Epileptic psychosis and feeblemindedness	12
Affective psychosis	7
Schizophreniform psychosis	25
Neurological diseases	5
Others	23

Table 3.4
Case of Margarethe P.

Original	*Translation*
Gegen Revers am 4. Aug. entlassen, kam sie am 15. Sept. mit Parere Dr. Moser wieder, welches die Angabe macht, "daß sie schreit, tobt, Geld zum Fenster hinaus wirft, niemanden zu sich läßt." Sie soll erst seit den letzten 14 Tagen erregt sein, Medikamente verweigern. Auf der Klinik ganz unzugänglich.	Released on August 4th, she came back on September 15th with admission papers by Dr. Moser who says that she cries, is in a rage, throws her money about, does not let anybody near to her. She is said to have been excited and to have refused her medicine for a fortnight only. At the clinic totally unapproachable.

mentally ill?—Yes—Dangerous to himself or others? Or at least disturbing other people?—Yes—In which way?—By excitement and paranoid ideas—Is he/she to be taken to an asylum?—Yes—Is the disease curable?—No answer—In which way shall the patient be transported?—By horse-drawn coach. Signed "Dr.Freud"/ "vidi Meynert."

Margarethe P. was taken to the Asylum of Lower Austria, where she remained for another two months. The case history from the asylum is much more detailed than Freud's in respect to the inner world of this patient and the development of her illness. She remained very aggressive and was often in a rage. She would not leave the hospital when her mother came to take her home. To a psychiatrist of our day with some knowledge of psychoanalytic theory there is much reason to believe that psychological mecha-

Table 3.5
Case of Josef J.

Original	Translation
Prüf<un>g auf Aphasie:	*Aphasia examination*
Federstiel: Spanfeder, die werden jedenfalls zum . . . verwandt sein, verwenden, zum schreiben.	*Quill:* pen, is used for . . . to use, is used for writing.
Kerze: Wachskerz	*Candle:* wax candle.
Streusandbüchse: Das sind meine Sachen, a mit [. . .] ist das, das ist, was sie jetzt geschrieben haben. Ja, essen kann i's net.	*Writing sand box:* these are my things, a . . . , that's what you just wrote down. I can't eat it.
Tintenzeug: Das ist auch so eine zweideutige Geschicht, Höll oder was.	*Ink pot:* that's also an ambiguous thing, hell or what.
Glas u. Streusandbüchse: richtig	*Glass and writing sand box:* correctly.
Messer: das weiß ich selber nicht— das wird nur geschliffen u. zusammengesteckt,—ja freilich, so wird geschnitten, es gehört zum Schneiden.	*Knife:* I don't know, it's being whet and put together, oh yes, it's for cutting.

nisms were at work in this woman's illness. For Freud in 1883, however, and under the work conditions at Meynert's clinic, it was obviously impossible to plunge into the dynamics of such cases.

In contrast to these case histories there are a few case reports from which we can get an inkling of Freud's talent for clinical observation. All of these patients suffered from organic brain diseases. Just one example: on 2 May a thirty-four-year-old patient[18] was admitted to the clinic. He suffered from headaches and insomnia. He was restless and confused. When he arrived, he had a fever, tachycardia, meningism, and aphasia. Freud carefully documented the psychic and somatic states, including a very extended aphasia examination. Some thirty different objects were shown to the patient, and Freud transcribed his answers (table 3.5). What we see is a very vivid picture of a case of sensory aphasia. In the following days, the patient's condition worsened, and on 8 May at 5:30 A.M., he died. The autopsy confirmed that he had suffered from tubercular meningitis.

Just a few hours later another patient[19] was transferred to the clinic from an internal ward. He suffered from rabies and was so violently excited that he had to be firmly bound to a stretcher. He was administered huge doses of morphine and chloral hydrate, but died the next afternoon. Freud wrote down his case history immediately afterwards. This report shows the fluent, clear, gripping language we know from many of Freud's works.

Let us summarize what we can learn from the case histories about Freud's daily work at Meynert's clinic. The great majority of the case reports are rather superficial. Documentation of mental status seldom corresponds to what was recommended in textbooks at that time, while the somatic state is often documented with much greater sophistication. Diagnoses seldom show critical reflection— rather they seem primarily to justify measures to be taken. Only a few cases show that the writer was familiar with the scientific discussions of his time. Freud seems considerably removed from his patients.

At the same time, a few cases of special brain diseases are different in style and character and more precisely documented. In these Freud's interest and personal involvement can be seen much more clearly.

Freud's Personal Situation

We have seen that the circumstances at Meynert's clinic were more than difficult for Freud and his work. But are those circumstances really sufficient to explain fully why he did not engage himself in psychiatry? Should a man as highly gifted as Freud not be able to come to grips with strenuous external situations? Others have gone through the arduous first months at psychiatric hospitals without giving up quickly. We need to take into consideration another important factor, namely Freud's own personal situation during those months. We know from the available biographical material—a few published letters to his wife Martha and others quoted by Jones— that Freud himself underwent a personal crisis during those months. Martha moved to Wandsbeck near Hamburg in June 1883. For many weeks he felt deeply depressed and irritated and doubted the value of their relationship as well as his own ability to be a good doctor. I am quite sure that we will learn some more about his feelings when the unpublished Martha letters are made fully available. His situation slowly stabilized in the autumn of 1883, after he had already left Meynert's clinic. His difficulties with Martha had lessened; he had some success in his laboratory work; he had gained more self-confidence. The following year his scientific work found some appreciation, and he became interested in and enthusiastic about the therapeutic value of cocaine. In 1885 he finished his university qualification as a *Privatdozent* for diseases of the nervous system and received a grant to study under Charcot for a few months. In Paris, Freud became familiar with Charcot's dynamic understanding of the functional disturbances of the nervous system. It was this concept that was to influence his own way of thinking more deeply than any other in the next years. Only with this dynamic conception of neurosis was he able to develop a theory of psychiatric phenomena, as he did when he subsumed paranoia under the "neuropsychoses of defense."

Could Freud have gone a different way? Could he have become a neuropsychiatrist? What would have happened to his ideas if he had established himself at Meynert's clinic? Freud clearly felt that the psychiatric path would lead him into an impasse. It sounds paradoxical, but it was due to the extreme orientation of Meynert's psychiatric system, the deplorable circumstances of his clinic, the unhappy personal situation of both Meynert and Freud, and above all the extremely difficult patients with their often hopeless states of illness that enabled Freud to find his own way and leave clinical psychiatry behind him. With the help of Charcot and Breuer he was able to hone his vision and develop a model to understand hysteria, and only after a long detour did he come to a dynamic understanding also of the severe mental disorders he faced in the psychiatric wards.

Notes

1. Freud to Bleuler, 30 January 1906; cf. Bleuler 1983, 159.
2. Freud 1925d, 87; cf. *S.E.* 20:61 (the French expression in Freud's German text was here replaced by "peaceful penetration").
3. Freud to Hollós, 4 October 1928, in Schur 1966, 21f.

4. Eissler 1974, 65–67.
5. Gicklhorn and Gicklhorn 1960.
6. Eissler 1966.
7. Hirschmüller 1989.
8. Jaspers 1973, 705ff.
9. Cr. Marx 1971.
10. Stockert-Meynert 1930, 76.
11. Meynert 1884; English trans., 1885.
12. Cf. Schulz 1977, 132.
13. Stone 1971.
14. Wolf 1973.
15. Hirschmüller 1989, case report no. 12.
16. Ibid., case report no. 3.
17. Ibid., case report no. 41/79.
18. Ibid., case report no. 8.
19. Ibid., case report no. 14.

References

Bleuler, E. 1983. *Lehrbuch der Psychiatrie.* 15th ed., revised by Manfred Bleuler. Berlin, Heidelberg, and New York: Springer-Verlag.
Eissler, K. R. 1966. *Sigmund Freud und die Wiener Universität. Über die Pseudowissenschaftlichkeit der jüngsten Wiener Freud-Biographik.* Bern and Stuttgart: Huber.
———. 1974. Gedenkrede zur 30. Wiederkehr von Sigmund Freuds Todestag. *Jahrb. Psychoanal.* 7:23–75.
Freud, S. 1925. An autobiographical study. *S.E.* 20:7–74.
Gicklhorn, J., and Gicklhorn, R. 1960. *Sigmund Freuds akademische Laufbahn im Lichte der Dokumente.* Vienna and Innsbruck: Urban & Schwarzenberg.
Hirschmüller, A. 1989. *Die Wiener Psychiatrie der Meynert-Zeit. Untersuchungen zu Sigmund Freuds nervenarztlicher Ausbildung.* Tübingen: Habilitationschrift Theor. Med.
Jaspers, K. 1973. *Allgemeine Psychopathologie.* 9th ed. Berlin, Heidelberg, and New York: Springer-Verlag.
Marx, O. M. 1971. Psychiatry on a neuropathological basis: Th. Meynert's application for the extension of the venia legendi. *Clio Med.* 6:139–158.
Meynert, T. 1884. *Psychiatrie. Klinik der Erkrankung des Vorderhirns, begründet auf dessen Bau, Leistungen und Ernährung.* Vienna: Braumüller.
———. 1885. *Psychiatry: A clinical treatise on diseases of the forebrain, based upon a study of its structure, functions, and nutritio.* Trans. by B. Sachs. Part 1: The anatomy, physiology, and chemistry of the brain. New York and London: Putnam's Sons.

Schulz, F. 1977. *Prof. Dr. Th. Meynert und seine gehirnanatomischen und psychiatrischen Arbeiten 1863–1892*. Vienna: Self-published.

Schur, M. 1966. *The Id and the Regulatory Principles of Mental Functioning*. New York: International Universities Press.

Stockert-Meynert, D. 1930. *Theodor Meynert und seine Zeit. Zur Geistesgeschichte Österreichs in der 2. Hälfte des 19. Jahrhunderts*. Vienna and Leipzig: Österreicher Bundesverlag.

Stone, I. 1971. *The Passions of the Mind*. New York: Doubleday and Co.

Wolf, E. S. 1973. Minister to a mind diseased: Freud at the Allgemeine Krankenhaus. *Annual Psychoanaly*. 1:336–341.

4

Metapsychology and Consciousness: Discussion of Albrecht Hirschmüller's Presentation

Elio J. Frattaroli

The NIMH has declared the 1990s to be the decade of the Brain. Psychiatric residents are currently being taught how to monitor drug levels in the blood and make diagnoses by questionnaire, but not how to listen and talk to human beings or how to think about the human mind. Those who do not remember the past are condemned to repeat it, and so we find ourselves confronted with a new edition of Meynert's neuropathologically based psychiatry, the same psychiatry that Freud found so barren more than a century ago. I hope that Dr. Hirschmüller's valuable contribution will help us to remember Meynert's failure and recognize the barrenness of our own psychiatry so that we can emulate Freud in moving beyond naive biological reductionism to a fuller understanding of the human mind. But there is a problem with this hopeful scenario. Not everyone agrees that Freud ever really did move beyond reductionism. In the burgeoning field of Freud studies, many scholars now contend that Freud's well-known shift from brain to mind was more apparent than real, that he remained throughout his psychoanalytic career a "crypto-biologist," and that psychoanalytic theory is based on the mistaken physicalistic premises he inherited from Meynert, Brücke, and others.[1] This view represents a profound misconception of the nature of psychoanalysis, a misconception that I will try to dispel in this discussion.

Imagine that you are a scientist with dreams of making an epochal discovery. Picture yourself feverishly adjusting the lenses of your microscope, trying to bring into focus a blurry object which you know to be of vital importance and which has never before been adequately visualized or described. The object is alive and elusive, but gradually it seems to be gaining definition under your microscope. Then just as you are making the final adjustments that should bring it clearly into focus, it vanishes. This is, I believe, a fairly accurate metaphorical account of Freud's experience in writing his "Psychology for Neurologists," known to us as the *Project for a Scientific Psychology* (1895). The object under his microscope was the human mind. The microscope was the conceptual framework of neuroscience.

Freud's experience is typical of what happens when we try to apply narrow explanatory categories and methods to a domain of experience that transcends them. For instance, Niels Bohr (1958) has pointed out that if we attempt to apply the experimental methods of chemistry and physics to the study of the living organism we will inevitably kill the organism in the process. Life vanishes under the microscope of physical science, because the phenomenon of life transcends the phenomena of chemistry and physics. Similarly, the methods of neurophysiology cannot be applied to the study of mental processes without altering or obliterating the consciousness that is to be studied. The phenomenon of consciousness transcends the phenomena of neurophysiology, and so it vanishes under the microscope of neuroscience. Mind can in principle never be explained in terms of brain processes.

This was certainly not the position of Meynert, for whom psychopathology was solely a consequence of physiologic dysfunction in the brain. Meynert's approach exemplifies what Bertram Lewin (1946) has called "medical countertransference": a carrying over of the emotional detachment of the gross anatomy laboratory into the physician's attitude toward living patients, along with the wish that all patients might be as tractable as that first patient, the cadaver. According to Lewin, "the heat which rises from so many useless clashes between the proponents of 'organic' and 'psychological' medicine might not appear, if it were realized that the main issue was a matter of preference, an emotional preference for the dead or the live patient" (p. 197). It might be said that Freud's shift from neuropathology to psychoanalysis was a shift from interest in the dead patient, who can best be understood through autopsy material, to interest in the living patient, who can best be understood through introspective and empathic awareness of immediate lived experience.

Dr. Hirschmüller helps us understand the roots of this shift in Freud's disillusionment with Meynert's deadening approach to patients. But it was not until more than a decade later, when he abandoned his unfinished *Project for a Scientific Psychology*, that Freud finally gave up for good the attempt to look at the mind through Meynert's microscope, recognizing that it was as futile as trying to take a photograph of a dream. He made the transition from the brain of the *Project* to the mind of *The Interpretation of Dreams* (1900) because the intractability of the *Project* had forced him to acknowledge the inherent limits on reductionism and the unavoidable epistemological dualism these limits entail. As he put it in the opening paragraph of the *Outline of Psychoanalysis* (1940):

We know two kinds of things about what we call our psyche (or mental life): firstly, its bodily organ and scene of action, the brain (or nervous system) and, on the other hand, our acts of consciousness, which are immediate data and cannot be further explained by any sort of description. Everything that lies between is unknown to us, and the data do not include any direct relation between these two terminal points of our knowledge. If it existed, it would at the most afford an exact localization of the processes of consciousness and would give us no help towards understanding them.

Freud is unambiguously dualistic here, identifying two epistemological "terminal points" or bottom lines: brain and consciousness. The categories used to understand and the terms used to describe brain states are simply not applicable to states of consciousness. Mind must be understood on its own psychological terms, that is, in terms that refer ultimately to acts of consciousness.

It is especially noteworthy that Freud identifies consciousness, and not the Unconscious, as the terminal point in our knowledge of the psyche. The Unconscious may be the bottom line of motivation, but consciousness is the bottom line of observation. Indeed, we can only know of unconscious motives to the extent that they produce manifestations in someone's consciousness. Dreams may be the royal road to the Unconscious, but they are, in themselves, acts of consciousness. In fact, all the hard data of psychoanalysis are acts of consciousness—specifically, acts of introspection and empathy.

Thus, although it is not usually thought of in this way, psychoanalysis can properly be described as the scientific study of consciousness. The transition from Meynert's psychiatry to Freud's psychoanalysis was a transition from the extrospective study of the brain to the introspective study of acts of consciousness. I emphasize this fact because it is precisely the failure to appreciate the centrality of consciousness in psychoanalytic observation that has led to the misunderstanding of psychoanalysis as a "crypto-biological" pseudo-science.

This misunderstanding has unfortunately been fostered by our own psychoanalytic literature, which until recently has too often seemed to prefer the dead patient to the living, reading like a dissection manual or an autopsy report when it should read like a novel, vastly overemphasizing metapsychology while describing very little of what actually happens in the consciousness of patient and analyst during a psychoanalytic hour. Many of the Freud scholars who misconstrue psychoanalysis as a reductionistic theory know it only through this literature. They have no firsthand experience of the subtle flow and unfolding of consciousness in free association or of the resonance of countertransference when it is captured as an awareness just on the edge of enactment.

To a practicing psychoanalyst, and to a psychoanalytic patient, the most convincing proof of a clinical hypothesis comes when an unconscious feeling that could previously only be inferred becomes a conscious experience that the patient can acknowledge and describe. Where *It* was, there *I* shall become. In this process of emergence into consciousness, an aspect of self that had previously been disowned via repression is clearly observed for the first time and recognized as belonging to self. This observational process depends not at all on metapsychology or on neurobiological premises.

Those who view psychoanalysis as reductionistic or crypto-biological misunderstand the nature of psychoanalytic observation and its relation to metapsychology. They start from the fact that many of Freud's later metapsychological ideas have precursors in the neurobiological model of the *Project*. They argue that Freud never really abandoned this model, but simply translated it from a language that was explicitly physicalistic to one that was implicitly so. They then lump together the *Project*'s neurobiology and the metapsychology that seems to be modeled after it, and take them to represent an a priori reductionistic program, like that of Meynert, which they claim is the fundamental paradigm of psychoanalysis. Since the conceptual paradigm of the observer necessarily influences what can be observed, they claim further that the supposedly psychological observations of the consulting room are actually disguised and deformed derivatives of Freud's a priori physicalist assumptions.

It is true that the metapsychology evolved out of what I would call the metaneurology of the *Project*. However, it is putting the epistemological cart before the horse to assume that these "meta"-theories constitute a conceptual framework that precedes clinical observation. Although Freud acknowledged that all observation must necessarily be conditioned by some a priori premises, he nevertheless maintained that the metapsychology did not have such a priori status for psychoanalytic observations. Metapsychological concepts, according to Freud, "are not the foundation of science, upon which everything rests: that foundation is observation alone. They are not the bottom but the top of the whole structure, and they can be replaced and discarded without damaging it" (1914, 77).

The observations Freud refers to here are the introspective and empathic observations of subjective experience, acts of consciousness, made available through the psychoanalytic method. That he puts them at the foundation of psychoanalytic science does not imply that these observations are unconditioned by underlying a priori assumptions; only that the underlying assumptions in question are not those of the metapsychology. What is a priori for psychoanalysis is not, for instance, the metapsychological assumption that cathexis needs to be discharged, but the implicit mentalist assumption that emotions need to be expressed. It is this latter assumption that informed Breuer's and Freud's early work with hypnosis, catharsis, and the talking cure. It continues to inform psychoanalytic work today, although we might now place less emphasis on the importance of a cathartic expression of emotion and more on the importance of a full inner experience of emotion.

Those who see in the parallels between the *Project* and the metapsychology evidence that psychoanalysis is grounded in materialist premises miss the crucial fact that even in the *Project* Freud started from introspectively based psychological observations and the preconceived mentalistic premises they entailed. He then tried to imagine what might be going on in the neurones to account for the mental phenomena (such as memory, repression, consciousness, etc.) for which he already had a preliminary mentalistic account. For instance, the observational fact was that an idea can be experienced with great emotional intensity. The abstraction, or metaphor, for this observation was that a neurone can be "cathected" with a large quantity of energy. The mentalistic concept of an "idea" in association with other "ideas" came first. Freud then created the physicalistic metaphor of a cathected neurone (corresponding to an idea) in contact with other neurones via conduction pathways (corresponding to associative links). The physicalist picture of distinct groupings of phi and psi neurones did not come from Freud's neuroanatomic observations. It came from his introspective observation that as a subjective experience, memory differs from perception. Throughout the *Project*, Freud's physicalistic account of neuronal mechanisms is a secondary elaboration, an abstract description of psychological experience first conceptualized in mentalistic terms and grounded in mentalistic premises.[2]

It would be absurd to argue that when, in the *Project*, Freud equates symbol formation with the motion of neuronal quantity, he is deriving his sense of what symbol formation is from presuppositions about the flow of neuronal charge. It is equally absurd, for the same reasons, to argue that Freud's metapsychology is derived from his neurology. The metaneurology of the *Project* was simply the first version of the metapsychology, and it was derived, like the later versions, as an abstraction or metaphor for an autonomously mentalistic psychology.

It is incumbent on those who argue that Freud's psychology is based on neurological presuppositions to show how those presuppositions influenced the development of his psychological concepts. For instance, can it be shown that Freud would never have conceived of repression as he did if it weren't for his preconceptions about brain functioning? Quite the opposite. He would never have conceived of neuronal function as he did in the *Project* if not for his mentalistic presuppositions about repression. The notion of repression derived from the mentalistic understanding of subjective experiences, namely hypnosis, catharsis, and the talking cure, and not from Freud's model of brain functioning.

This is not to deny that there is a current of materialistic reductionism in Freud's work. In some moods and at some times Freud wished there could be a neurological bedrock from which psychological concepts might be derived, and indeed he imagined himself to be discovering such a bedrock while he was writing the *Project*. But from the beginning there was also a strong organismic mentalist current in Freud's thought, which gave him the perspective to recognize finally that what he had imagined himself to be doing in the *Project* simply could not be done.

It is widely assumed that, because Freud was trained by Brücke and Meynert and expressed admiration for both of them, he must have been imbued with their materialist philosophy and taken it as his own. Not only is this assumption inconsistent with Freud's manifest and explicit dualism, as I have tried to show, but it is also highly implausible on more general grounds. For one thing, Freud's intellectual and cultural background was highly diverse and included strong humanist nonreductionist influences such as Brentano and Goethe, whose pantheistic essay on nature first inspired Freud to study medicine.[3]

For another, it is a fact of human development that ideas, including underlying philosophical assumptions, change from generation to generation, a process on which Freud commented as follows (see Jones 1949, 75–76):

The detachment of the growing individual from the authority of the parents is one of the most necessary, but also one of the most painful, achievements of development. It is absolutely necessary for it to be carried out, and we may assume that every normal human being has to a certain extent managed to achieve it. Indeed, the progress of society depends in general on this opposition of the two generations.

It is a central discovery of psychoanalysis that this intergenerational process is subtended by an intrapsychic one, which we call the Oedipal conflict. At the intergenerational level there is a Hegelian dialectic in which the thesis of one generation gives birth to its antithesis in the next. At the intrapsychic level, both thesis and antithesis are represented, and constitute the two poles of the Oedipal conflict. The work of any creative thinker will reveal a tension between these two poles, the *conservative* pole representing the intellectual/cultural assumptions of the milieu in which the thinker was educated, and the *progressive* pole representing what is original and "countercultural" in his or her thought. Creativity depends on the progressive, "antithetical" forces being strong enough to break or transcend the constraints of the old weltanschauung or paradigm. It is the universality of this process that helps give to Michelangelo's *Prisoners*, struggling to break free from the inarticulate marble, their emblematic power. How utterly implausible then the notion that one of the major creative thinkers in human history never emerged from the marble of Meynert's narrow thought.

Michelangelo's prisoners provide a fitting image on which to close this discussion. Not only can they stand as emblem for Freud's struggle toward a psychoanalytic synthesis that would transcend the constraints of Meynert's reductionistic psychiatry. They also stand as emblem for the psychoanalytic process itself, for the conflicted unfolding of consciousness out of unconsciousness, for the emergence of an I out of an It.

Notes

1. Representative of this position are Sulloway (1979) and Mackay (1989).
2. This view is consistent with that of Kanzer (1973).
3. See Kaufmann (1980), and Gedo and Pollock (1976), for a discussion of humanistic influences in Freud's education.

References

Bohr, N. 1958. *Atomic Physics and Human Knowledge.* New York: John Wiley and Sons.

Freud, S. 1895. Project for a scientific psychology. *S.E.* 1:295–387.

———. 1900. The interpretation of dreams. *S.E.* 4 and 5.

———. 1914. On narcissism: An introduction. *S.E.* 14:67–102.

———. 1940. An outline of psycho-analysis. *S.E.* 23:141–208.

Gedo, J., and Pollock, G., eds. 1976. *Freud: The Fusion of Science and Humanism.* New York: International Universities Press.

Jones, E. 1949. *Hamlet and Oedipus.* New York: W. W. Norton, 1976.

Kanzer, M. 1973. Two prevalent misconceptions about Freud's "Project" (1895). *Annual of Psychoanalysis* 1:88–103.

Kaufmann, W. 1980. *Discovering the Mind,* vol. 3: *Freud versus Adler and Jung.* New York: McGraw-Hill.

Lewin, B. 1946. Counter-transference in the technique of medical practice. *Psychosomatic Medicine* 8:195–199.

Mackay, N. 1989. *Motivation and Explanation: An Essay on Freud's Philosophy of Science.* Madison, Conn.: International Universities Press.

Sulloway, F. 1979. *Freud, Biologist of the Mind.* New York: Basic Books.

5

Freud's View of Mental Health and Fate

Albert J. Solnit

In 1900 Sigmund Freud, a Viennese neurologist, was in the throes of discovering psychoanalysis as a systematic study of man's subjective experiences and the influence of those subjective states on man's behavior and on his view of himself and his personal relationships. At that time he wrote to his friend and corresponding colleague Wilhelm Fliess: "I am not a man of science at all, not an observer, not an experimenter, not a thinker. I am nothing but a conquistador by temperament, an adventurer if you want to translate this term, with all the inquisitiveness, daring and tenacity of such a man."[1] According to Ernest Jones, Freud's search for knowledge and truth became the driving force of his life: "His mind was not of the philosophic or contemplative kind, it was a restlessly inquiring mind."[2]

In 1914 Freud indicated that it was his fate "to agitate the sleep of mankind," and in 1925 he wrote to the novelist Stefan Zweig that the fundamental task of psychoanalysis was to "struggle with the demon," the demon of man's irrationality, in a "sober way" as a "comprehensible object of science."[3] Indeed, Freud took considerable pride in being the destroyer of illusions, the faithful servant of scientific veracity. In 1910 he wrote that "the truth is for me the absolute aim of science." In 1932, toward the end of his life, he wrote to Albert Einstein in the famous correspondence, *Why War?* that "I no longer count as one of my merits that I always tell the truth as much as possible; it has become my metier."

In Freud's own words, in his autobiography written in 1925, we gain direct access to how this genius of the late nineteenth and early twentieth century saw himself:

I was born on May 6, 1856, at Freiberg in Moravia, a small town in what is now Czechoslovakia. My parents were Jews, and I have remained a Jew myself. . . . When I was a child of four, I came to Vienna, and I went through the whole of my education there. At the "Gymnasium" I was at the top of my class for 7 years; I enjoyed special privileges there and was required to pass scarcely any examinations. Although we lived in very limited circumstances, my father insisted that, in my choice of a profession, I should follow my own inclinations alone. Neither at that time, nor indeed in my later life, did I feel any particular predilection for the career of a doctor. I was moved, rather, by a sort of curiosity, which was, however, directed more towards human concerns than towards natural objects; nor had I grasped the importance of observation as one of the best means of gratifying it. My deep engrossment in the Bible story (almost as soon as I had learnt the art of reading) had, *as I recognized much later*, an enduring effect upon the direction of my interest. (my emphasis)[4]

I will divide the remainder of this lecture into two sections. In the first part I will indicate, illustratively, how Freud's discoveries of the unconscious, of infantile sexuality, and of the interpretation of dreams and psychoanalytic treatment as a research method and as therapy have influenced the daily contemporary work of many therapists, teachers, and researchers. In the second part, I will use clinical examples to illustrate how Freud's concept of man as a historical creature underpins our assumption that each person's personality, uniqueness, and functioning cannot be well understood without understanding the connections between past experiences and current functioning. This suggests how each person is enabled to anticipate and prepare for the future. This emphasis also indicates the powerful thrust of Freud's discoveries on our studies of human development, especially child development.

Freud's greatest discoveries can be conceptualized under two headings. First is the systematic account of how man's unconscious feelings and thoughts influence his view of himself, his behavior and the choices he makes in regard to his friends and lovers, work, value preferences, and so on. Within this area we should ask: "Is a person responsible for his or her unconscious feelings, thoughts, and motivations?" Freud demonstrated that psychoanalysis enables each individual to accept responsibility for the choices he makes. The more the individual is able to make conscious what had been unconscious, the more he or she can take charge of his or her own life. In this way, Freud's charting of the inner life, the subjective experiences of the individual, has left us with a method and the scope of its influence.

Second, Freud carefully pointed out in how many ways each person's uniqueness reflects how past experiences and attitudes influence present and future behavior and expectations. Thus Freud's discovery of psychoanalysis also made it clear that each person has a unique history that must be taken into account in order to understand the developing person in the present and future.

In summary, according to Freud's discoveries each adult is able to take charge of himself or herself in the past, present, and future. Human infants, born helpless, gradually move toward adult independence as they are nurtured, protected, and guided by affectionate adults. Parents take responsibility for their children until the children are able to take on adult functions, including accepting responsibility for himself or herself as a unique person with a unique history.

In ancient times all illness and disease was viewed in a fatalistic way, as the choice of the gods or bad spirits, but not as the choice of the suffering human beings. There were pestilences, catastrophes, and individual illnesses that were thought of as having been brought upon a person or a population group as a consequence of their evil or provocative behavior. This superstitious reasoning was also used in the service of prevention when a person or group of persons was sacrificed in order to ward off the anger or disapproval of those magical forces that resided in the power of the gods or spirits that were perceived as controlling the fate of men, women, and children.

This perspective on what determined the health or illness of human beings was eroded in the eighteenth and nineteenth centuries as man, dissatisfied with his feelings of helplessness, pressed his curiosity to an increased awareness of the causes of infections and malnutrition, reaching for rational levels of explanation. The basis of medicine changed gradually from mysticism to a more rational view, to the physiological and morphological approaches established by anatomists, pathologists, bacteriologists, and others who increasingly used logical knowledge, methods, and technical devices (microscopes, X-ray diagnostic machines, pharmacological agents, and the like) to describe the course and causes of many infectious and deficiency diseases.

However, in the mental health field, despite great advances starting with Sigmund Freud toward the end of the nineteenth century,[5] we have continued to struggle with how to describe and how to understand the causes, the course, and the therapy of psychiatric disorders.

Fate or Choice?

By making conscious what had been unconscious, we are able to be more aware of our choices and their consequences. For example, does the fear and resentment of the menopause feel like a fate that cannot be avoided? How should one cope with the inevitability of biological changes that are part of our equipmental template? Can one accept oneself as an autonomous person without submitting to the illusion that our fate is outside of our control? Can one cope without resigning? Freud believed that the freedom to think, to know, to remember, to make conscious what had been unconscious (repressed, forgotten) was a sign of mental health that enabled the individual to know what choices were available given the individual's physical and mental resources and his unique history.

Often the thinking of nonprofessionals and even professionals includes a strong superstitious belief that mental illness represents the stigmatizing hand of fate, side by side with the rational knowledge of what constitutes and causes mental illness. Over and over again, professionals who are very knowledgeable about affective disorders or the schizophrenias will confide that, personally, they feel the person earned this by some wrongdoing. Thus they take a moralistic or superstitious stance while also using their sophisticated rational knowledge in understanding mental illness.

Our colleagues in medicine—pediatricians and surgeons as well as the other specialists, have urged us to use the same criteria for answering those questions of etiology, natural history, and therapy of mental illness that they have found so productive in revealing the explanations about infectious, degenerative, neoplastic, traumatic, and congenital disorders or deviant conditions. These criteria include the experimental replicability of the condition, in animals where possible; the description of the morphological and physiological characteristics of the condition—the detailed account of the agent of the illness, ranging from microorganisms to chemical descriptions of the deficiency or the deviant substances involved, to experimental surgical or pharmacological correction or amelioration, to genetic transmissibility where appropriate; and studies of random samples of the population that allow us to use scientific epidemiological knowledge and methods in describing the incidence, transmission, and fluctuation of the condition, as well as the associated variables involved.

In this way, studies have been carried out to tighten the explanatory connections between etiological agents or causes, susceptible or invulnerable states of those at risk and the effects of surgical, pharmacological, or replacement therapies. Currently we can see that certain interphases between physical and psychological medicine are beginning to be quite productive. For example, in the field of immunology more and more research will be conducted to examine psychologically and biologically what we mean by states of susceptibility and states of invulnerability.

In mental illness these scientific research methods are useful, especially for the major psychiatric disorders of psychoses and the related conditions. However, even in conditions that are commonly associated with psychiatric hospitalization, we struggle to understand to what degree people are biologically predisposed and to what degree it is their social environments and experiences that determine why a particular patient suffers from schizophrenia, manic-depressive states, major depressive conditions, and so on.

Certainly, we can all agree that nature and nurture are *always* intricately interwoven and involved.

In outlining the criteria for healthy psychological development, we view social development as a composite of psychological, emotional, intellectual, and physical factors. Perceptual, motoric, emotional, and intellectual functioning take place and are assessed in a social-historical context.

In the newborn period, the infant's rhythm and characteristics of sleeping, eating, and fussing as well as its reactions to affection, soothing, frustration, discomfort, and so forth are key reactions in determining normative or healthy functioning. The newborn who cannot be aroused easily or who is difficult to soothe, that is, whose normative opportunities are associated with difficult choices, may be giving early warning signs of significant developmental difficulties which may later lead to the discovery of either environmental or biological deficits. It is not unusual, however, for biological and environmental influences to complement each other. In fact, normative constitutional and environmental factors that fit well usually promote healthy development; for example, the competent mother responding with ease and satisfaction to a vigorous, demanding newborn usually leads to healthy mutual adaptation, whereas the same active infant behavior sometimes evokes conflicted and confusing reactions in less adaptive mothers who react by placing obstacles in the path of healthy child development. That is, a mother who is uncertain and anxious may be easily upset by the normative demands of a vigorous baby. This mother may function more adequately and confidently with a more placid infant. In a slightly different context, there are some parents who, because of their past experiences, feel more competent, especially with a first baby, in caring for a child of one sex rather than the other. Such opportunities and choices may become patterned over time through repeated interactions.

With our advancing technology, for example in the use of amniocentesis, we often have early knowledge about the sex of an unborn child. With such knowledge, will people decide to make choices about the sex of a wanted child? In some communities have there been abortions carried out because the child was not of the preferred sex? This could be a tragic dilemma in which choices may say more about fate than our wisdom can sustain. What if this dilemma is qualified in certain cases, such as when the fetus is male and the child would suffer because it carries a lethal gene, but if it is female it will be spared the lethal sex-linked gene?

Through an older child's developing capacities to defer the demands of the instinctual drives—that is, the impulsive, appetitive need, to transform the drives and to accept partial and substitutive gratifications—the child is assured of sound social capacities and satisfactions as well as a realistic self-esteem. By being able to master physical and mental challenges and by being able to form empathetic personal relationships, the child acquires the ability to persist—even in the face of adversity—in efforts to influence or change the social and physical environment.

In this context, socializing is the bedrock for developmental health. If there is balance in the individual's efforts to find personal satisfactions and adapt to his or her social situation, then the child can become an adult who works productively and establishes satisfactory personal and social relationships. This concept of mental health is based on the assumption that a child's passive experiences (for example, being fed or bathed) can eventually be performed by himself or herself in an active and responsible way (for example, self-feeding and bathing). Increasingly, the child learns to take charge of its body and environment. Such active competent behavior also represents a choice. For such development to be optimally successful, the passive experience must be gratifying and conducted in an atmosphere of certain social expectations. That is, the mother not only enables the child to enjoy the feeding and bathing, but she takes satisfaction in enabling it to become independent of her as the child's unfolding capacities permit it to organize and make its own choices. The social context in which passive-to-active development takes place is crucial in facilitating or discouraging the healthy balance between the individual's adaptation to social realities and his or her efforts to change that environment. In healthy development the social environment also represents the uniqueness of those persons who constitute that child's human society.

Education that begins with pre-kindergarten schools is a highly desirable preparation for subsequent education and social development. Separation experiences in these schools are also helpful in assisting the child to exercise its capacities to identify with its parents as he or she learns to function as a member of a group in which the teacher is the guiding, protecting adult. Through repeated experiences with parents and siblings, the child internalizes their influence and adapts, in a unique way, many family attitudes and symbolizing activities for his or her own use. Primary relationships in the family enable the child to form new secondary relationships with teachers, peers, and others in a selective and discriminating manner. The absence of selectivity or discrimination in the formation of nursery-school friendships is usually a sign of developmental difficulties.

In the context of opportunities to develop interests in contemporaries through small peer groups and aided by the gradual domination of the tyrannical or compelling demands of his or her impulses and instinctual drives, the child gradually begins to develop its own ideals and values. The youngster will view the teacher, school, and class as uniquely related to himself or herself, and will invest much in learning about a larger social scene through the use of symbolic communications mastered through the child's progressive development. In this period, social meaning and values are implicit in the cognitive as well as in the play and social activities of the school. Thought becomes a trial of action. Such mental activity appears in many forms, including fantasy, memory, and planning (anticipatory thinking), which enlarge and enrich the child's contact with the social as well as the physical world. Increasingly, the child, and later the adolescent, is able to discern choices and to take responsibility for his or her own body and behavior.

When a healthy infant becomes a new member of a family I know personally, I often write to the "child", offering my congratulations on his or her selection of parents, especially when I know that the parents are strong adults with a firm, loving, and joyous commitment to children in an environment that is not economically, socially, or educationally impoverished. In that way I am trying to tell the parents that in making their choice to have a child they have given their son or daughter a desirable fate. In this instance the infant's fate represents a choice by the parents to have a child they can cherish and in whom they can find self-fulfillment. Professionals should be realistically respectful and admiring of the hard work involved for adults to nurture and support the growth and development of their child, which, after all, is satisfying evidence of their competence as parents. Unfortunately, some parents are overwhelmed by the demands of taking care of an infant or a young child and feel mistreated by fate. Such parents might say that it is their fate to have a child they cannot tolerate; some of them become child abusers. Other parents enjoy the child-rearing experience and feel liberated by their choice to have children. Such parents feel fulfilled and enlarged by their experience and gain self-understanding.

In the usual or average expectable environment, as children are able to become active in their own behalf, they gradually assume care of their own bodies. In this context their behavior is decisive; for example, when they are hungry, they cry. Initially, this is not a deliberate choice. It is a forerunner to what becomes a deliberate choice. A child who cries when it is hungry and has a mother or father who knows how to respond is in a position to develop the capacity for self-responsibility, even though the line between fate and choice may often seem blurred.

For example, an eleven-year-old boy, Tommy, was preoccupied with his mother's hysterectomy and depression. While she was convalescing at home, he was sent by her to purchase a loaf of bread. Despite a parental prohibition about riding his bicycle on a busy street, he decided to ride instead of walk to the nearby bakery. As he rode on the busy main street, he did not notice a truck drawing up on his right and turned right. He ran into the truck, was knocked off his bicycle, and incurred a fracture of his tibia, for which was hospitalized. Later on at the hospital he talked to me and to several others and told us how worried he was about his mother, and how he felt that maybe he had done something that had brought on her need for surgery. In a rather primitive way he connected his own birth with the idea that she had to have a hysterectomy, even though he was eleven by now and had two younger siblings. Later, he talked not only of the guilt of riding his bicycle on the busy street, but how he was so worried about his mother that he did not notice the truck pulling up. Was his accident a matter of choice or fate? As healing persons we should assume that his accident was in significant part a matter of Tommy's choice. In riding his bicycle he did what was forbidden because it was unsafe, choosing to take on risks that were heightened by his preoccupation about his mother's depressive reaction to knowing that she could not have another child.

Treatment enabled Tommy to understand why his leg was put in traction and later in a cast and why he should choose to cooperate with his treatment. The psychological treatment enabled Tommy to become aware of how he invited and allowed an accident to happen to him by disregarding an adult judgment about his safety on a busy thoroughfare, especially because in feeling upset about his mother's condition and in his preoccupation with her withdrawal from him (because of depression) he chose to disregard what was happening around him on a main street. He found himself yearning for closeness with his mother. As the treatment revealed, he symbolically and concretely identified with his mother, from whom he had been separated for ten days while she was in hospital for the surgery. Although he felt resentful about his mother's absence and "injury," he also felt he should have taken care of her but that he did not know how to do so. He felt punished for his dereliction.

Of course, that raises the complicated question: should a person take responsibility for his or her unconscious motivation? Do unconsciously motivated behaviors represent a choice, whether in accidents, psychoses, or neuroses? I do not hold that a murder by a psychotic person signifies that such a person is not guilty because of mental illness, nor do I hold that neurotic behavior should be viewed as fate, rather than choice, because of unconscious motivation. Logically, there can be no promise of therapeutic assistance in psychotic or neurotic patients unless the patients are able to understand that they are responsible for their behavior and for their development once they have passed their childhood. Therapeutic experience indicates that it is not until the person in treatment says, "Now I see what I did," that the therapist knows that the therapy is beginning to be useful to that patient. There is the risk that expecting patients to take responsibility for their behavior can be viewed moralistically by either the therapist or the patient. However, in therapy and in life, insight into how one may take responsibility for one's choices becomes a liberating experience rather than a guilt trip.

The following vignette illustrates "Human Development: Choice or Fate?"

Harry, thirty-five years old, married and the father of two children, sought treatment because of his repeated, unnecessary, destructive disputes with his boss in a middle-sized engineering firm. Psychoanalytic treatment revealed that he also suffered from a chronic marital difficulty. He felt his wife did not respect him. There were frequent outbursts in which he sulked, felt put down, and withdrew into spiteful, stony silences to the detriment of the marital relationship and with negative effects on his sons, who felt rejected by him.

In the psychoanalytic treatment, two lines of memory which he had been living out neurotically but did not remember were disclosed. The first was the recall of having been sick and confined to bed for six months at the age of thirteen. As he reconstructed the illness in his psychoanalytic treatment, he had been diagnosed as having a streptococcus infection. The family doctor had explained that he could damage his heart (probably he had rheumatic fever) if he did not remain in bed quietly for six months. He then brought up a clear memory of his father sternly warning him not to move or he would damage himself. As we examined the clarity of this new screening memory, the patient gradually realized that his mother and father had been very worried that he would be too restless in his sleep and had tied his hands and feet to the bed frame to keep him from moving. In the transference, he felt "tied down" by the analysis. He recalled his anger at his parents and his fear of damaging himself. Later in the analysis we were able to reconstruct his deep conviction that he had made himself sick through masturbation, associated with exciting fantasies of being overwhelmed by a strong woman, that is, of being forced to have sex with a woman.

Although this first line of recall was far from precise, it made sense to him and explained why he had been out of school for six months—a memory gap that had always puzzled him. It also led to his understanding why he was always trying to trap his boss into errors that led to anxious confrontations in which the patient felt put down, became compliant, and felt relieved and depressed.

In the next two years the patient's relationship to his boss gradually changed. He was promoted several times until he reached a managerial level that was highly satisfying and in which he now was the head of a large number of employees. He felt he was especially skilled in helping young "hell-raisers" when they entered the firm under his tutelage.

As he reached the end of his treatment, with improvement in his working capacities and satisfaction, he filled in further gaps in his memory. For the first time since adolescence, he recalled that when he returned to school, after six months of illness, he used to play basketball after school despite his father's threatening prohibition. The father had admonished him not to engage in any vigorous competitive sports because he had had an infection that might have weakened his heart. He remembered that he *had* to play, not only for the fun of it (he dearly loved and was highly skilled in such sports) but also because he was so anxious about falling ill again that in a counterphobic way he had to face the danger of competitive sports to find out if he was all right. Furthermore, he could not resist the pleasure he felt once he allowed himself to think of playing the game. In the analysis it was clear that playing basketball had at times also been equated with masturbation. As he would begin each game he felt a mounting irresistible pleasure and tension with anxiety. After the game he felt relief that he had not died or fallen ill again. Subsequently, after graduating high school and looking for work, he gave up sports. He chose what he felt would be a safe job that would not be too competitive. It was clear that he arranged for and accepted limits in his education and work that unconsciously he felt would offer safety and would avoid the danger of competition and greater satisfaction. In the analytic treatment it became clear that he felt that he had "damaged" himself and might damage himself further if he chose to be too ambitious or competitive.

The second line of remembering was the painful feeling that his father had preferred his older brother and that his mother, though more even in her affections, never took his side when the father and older brother seemed to gang up on him. This was reconstructed both in the transference (he was certain that the analyst preferred the older male patient who preceded him) and in clarifying his ongoing distortions of his relationship to his wife when he would perceive what he felt was her lack of respect for him. His sulkiness and stony silence were updated replicas of how he had acted when he felt let down by his father's preference for the brother, and especially because the mother did not seem to take his side. At those times he felt that no one really admired and cared for him.

As Harry recovered these memories and replaced unconsciously motivated destructive behavior at work and at home with the conscious memories of trauma and sense of deprivation, his recollections became worked through. He came to understand how he arranged to have his difficulties at work and at home; that he had been making choices about his way of shaping his personal relationships that served unconscious motives. These motives represented a neurotic residue of past burdens of trauma and deprivation. In his psychoanalytic treatment and in his life experiences, Harry learned that he could make other choices about his relationships once he was more aware of himself and how he behaved. Remembering liberated him. It enabled him to know the story of his life more coherently, though it did not provide him with a historically complete and accurate narrative about himself. He was able to feel in charge of himself and to gain relief from his persistent destructive behavior pattern at home and at work.

In using the psychoanalytic treatment process, Harry uncovered the gaps in his memory and gained a more coherent view of himself in his current situation and as a preparation for future life experiences. As Freud had predicted in 1912, the patient said, "Of course, I've always known about these matters, only I never thought about them."

In Harry's case, Loewald would say, "The movement from unconscious experience, from the instinctual life of the id to the reflective, purposeful life of the ego, means taking responsibility for one's own history, the history that has been lived and the history in the making."[6]

Ordinarily, Choice or Fate is a false dichotomy![7] It is always choice *and* fate. Fate is closer to biological and genetic endowment as well as to the environment into which one is born. Choice is closer to experience. The human social environment provides choices. Fate may set limits that cannot be breached. Choice enables the individual to exploit what is available within the limits of endowment, the environment into which one is born, and the nature of man-made catastrophes that one is subject to but which one did not choose or determine.

However, there is no effective psychotherapy possible—or at least only a very circumscribed degree of therapy—unless the patient, whether suffering from psychosis, neurosis, or developmental deviation (for example, maternal deprivation), takes responsibility for choices of behavior, including the voluntary choice of treatment. Fate and choice are inextricably interwoven into a fabric of experience and development. We accept realistic aspects of fate in order to stretch and shape it according to the choices we can make. We search for and embrace the opportunities to be aware of alternatives, selecting the most liberating choices that enable us to feel that we are living out our lives rather than to deceive ourselves into feeling we have no choice in how our lives unfold.

Notes

1. Peter Gay, *Freud: A Life for Our Time* (New York: W. W. Norton, 1988), p. xvi.
2. Ernest Jones, *Sigmund Freud: Four Centenary Addresses* (New York: Basic Books, 1956), p. 128.
3. Gay, *Freud*, p. xvii.
4. Freud, *An Autobiographical Study*, (S.E. 20:7–70, 1925).
5. Freud wrote that "after all, analysis does not set out to make pathological reactions impossible, but to give the patient's ego freedom to decide one way or the other" (*The Ego and the Id*, S.E. 19:12–59, 1923), p. 50 fn.
6. Loewald, H. *Psychoanalysis and the History of the Individual*, (New York & London: Yale University Press, 1978), p. 11.
7. In a world of the Holocaust or nuclear warfare, once let loose, there is no choice—only the fate of extinction. A fourteen-year-old has said: "I feel cheated. The future in which there can be nuclear war is no future—there are no choices."

6

Fate, Choice, and Retribution in Freud's Psychoanalysis

Howard H. Covitz

Some twenty-five years ago I was the student of Kazimierz Kura-
towski, who had produced the pioneering work in the area I was
then pursuing. His lectures struck me as an oddity: everyone could
understand them in spite of their depth. I was far more accustomed
as a graduate student to those who dazzled their audience with
fancy and technical footwork. Freud, too, had this same straightfor-
ward style of presentation; he addressed fundamental issues. His
cases, his papers, his letters were and are accessible to a broad
audience. His goal was not to obfuscate or to blind, but to clarify
and to elucidate the puzzles that came to confront us all after our
ancestors began to stand erect on the surface of this planet,
stripped of their protective instincts.

Just such a work is Albert Solnit's. He has written a chapter that—far away from technical metapsychological gambits—
challenges us in plain language to confront fundamental questions
in averring that the goal of psychoanalytic treatment is to let
Choice be where a sense of Fate once was, and to further suggest, in

his clinical vignettes, that Choice may not be something that is written in stone during the Oedipal and pre-Oedipal years alone, but rather an ego-function that is operational in an ongoing sense throughout life. My thoughts on this paper move in two directions: the notion of choice, on the one hand, and the issues concerning criminal responsibility, on the other. I begin with the matter of "choice."

In the case of young Tommy, the bicyclist, Dr. Solnit notes: "As healing persons we should assume that his accident was in significant part a matter of Tommy's choice . . . he did what was forbidden *because* it was unsafe, choosing to take on risks that were heightened by his preoccupation about his mother's depressive reaction" (my emphasis). Two issues have thus been raised. The first relates to whether or not the young fellow made a decision at the time of the accident; the second to those matters which may have prompted such a decision. While time does not permit a fair examination of Freud's thoughts on these matters as they developed from prepsychoanalytic models through the topographic and structural models, I offer some discrete thoughts about Freud's thinking.

In abandoning the Seduction Hypothesis, his position in the "Neuro-Psychoses of Defence" papers (1894 and 1896), Freud was assuredly not denying that children are abused in a variety of ways during childhood; the recent populist attackers of Freud present their material as if the Seduction Theory were equivalent to the statement "children are subject to destructive behaviors at the hands of their parents." (In his studies of Dora, the Rat Man, and the Wolf Man, Freud in no way seeks to hide the frequent presence of childhood seductions but rather, as Erikson (1962) noted to investigate genetic rather than historical reality. In giving up his "Neurotica," Freud reports struggling with the awareness that "in my case my father played no active role, though I certainly projected onto him an analogy from myself" (Kris 1954, 219). Not only the role of fantasy in psychic structure-building here saw its birth, but the activity of the child was here given life. Freud would have to grapple in the next decades with the child's fantasy-wish to have unilaterally dyadic relationships with each of the parents as well as the aggressive retributory strivings against all intruders to this Edenic bliss, that is, the complete Oedipal dilemma. The cause of neurosis was thereby shifted from the perverted fathers onto unconscious psychological solutions that their children ferreted out in response to their environment due to their own very special needs and demands.

Freud for forty years tackled this problem, attempting to respond to the question: *how* did the person under examination come to make the kind of choices he or she makes? The words "why" and "because" with their causative and implicitly accusatory denotations are rather alien to the historical etiologic model that Freud and his early students formulated. Many questions remain concerning not only young Tommy, but concerning the obsessional, the conversion hysteric, and virtually all other neurotics. Assuredly a decision is present in all such cases. But is this consideration germane to the task of the analyst? Freud postulated, and clearly and elegantly stated in his papers on metapsychology (Freud 1915a), that the unconscious is comprised of *Vorstellung*, visual scenarios, which canonically precipitate affects when these scenarios become conscious. He proposes that confusion and pathology arise when an affect is connected to an anaplastic or anachronistic scenario, one with which it should not expectedly attach. Here a proper, or ethical, choice is made quite difficult, if not impossible; the rule of the organism is to dispel such a foreign object, such an affect, in accordance with the principle that Freud posited very early in his work that allows the being to separate between internal and external stimuli, and which appears in his later works as the Constancy Principle, Nirvana Principle, and as various forms of the Pleasure Principle.

Certainly, as Dr. Solnit suggests, among the goals of psychoanalytic treatment is the eventual alteration of this state of affairs and its replacement with a mode of functioning that may not be *normal* but rather an improvement on the normal, with the introduction that psychoanalysis provides of a well-tuned associative function of the ego (Feldman, 1972).

The second matter, that of criminal responsibility, connects to the previous matter, that of choice. Just several years following Freud's introduction of the ubiquity of narcissism (an attempt to deal with the underlying "why?"), he suggested that the psychoanalytic theory of Unconscious Psychic Determination, which announces man's failure "to be supreme within his own mind," is a third blow that the "universal narcissism of men, their self love, has up to the present suffered . . . from the researches of Science" (Freud 1917, 284–285).

The heliocentrics—Copernicus, the Pythagoreans, and Aristarchus of Samos—had "declared that the earth was much smaller than the sun and moved around that celestial body." Then Darwin demonstrated that man "is not a being different from animals or superior to them; [being] himself of animal descent," and as Eissler would later note, a degradation, a fallen form, from the well-oiled instinct-guided animals to a drive-generated one. Freud continues noting that his "third blow, which is psychological in nature, is probably the most wounding" (p. 285).

Certainly it is the most unavoidable. Copernicus and Darwin can be and readily have been ignored by the method of incorporation or identification; the educated accept these scientific theories while—as is easily demonstrated by the manner in which they treat their world and their near kin in the animal kingdom—vitiating them. On the other hand, Freud's work that denies the comeliness of our everyday explanations is inescapable to all but the severely disturbed. Who among us has not sought, on some somnabulistic trek, to place blame for the stubbed toe on the offending night table or the sleeping spouse, while realizing, just a moment thereafter, the absurdity of such accusations? We are all made of such matter that seeks to deny culpability in actions.

Biblical characterology is rife with such behaviors. Adam blames "the woman you [God] gave to be with me" (Genesis III.12). Eve blames the "serpent who convinced me that I might eat" (III.13). It is interesting to note that while the capital crime of Onan (Genesis XXXVIII.9) is typically thought to be "spilling his seed upon the ground," a reading of the relevant passages leaves little doubt that Onan's failure to attend to family responsibility is at the center of his crime. He is presented as being narcissistically concerned with the fact that "not for him would be the seed" were he to fulfill the levirate for his dead brother. Cain, the exegetists would have it, sought to blame God for Abel's murder; God, he argued, had failed to teach him that stones would kill; God had placed the inclination toward evil in him; God had caused the argument in the first place by failing to accept a gift (Ginzburg 1920, 1:110). These exegetists then go on to note that Cain had no belief in these defenses.

Fifteen years ago, Eissler (1975), in what might be called a fourth blow to mankind's narcissism, convincingly argued that our cultural narcissism, beyond the individual narcissism that requires the above rationalizations, intrudes on our capacity to perceive realistically the unbridled destructive nature of our nations and our elected leaders, as well as impeding a realistic perception of our national documents, bringing humanity and its environs to the brink of disaster. Dr. Solnit, in his presentation, queries: "Should a person take responsibility for his or her unconcsious motivation? Do unconsciously motivated behaviors represent a choice, whether in accidents, psychoses or neuroses?" He goes on to answer: "I do not hold that a murder by a psychotic person signifies that such a peson is not guilty *because* of mental illness, nor do I hold that neurotic behavior should be viewed as fate, rather than choice, *because* of unconscious motivation" (my emphasis). Dr. Solnit's contributions are particularly timely in this era when the Seduction Hypothesis, and the multiple person psychologies that arise with it, are prevalent. By way of commentary, I should like briefly to examine the flip side of Dr. Solnit's comments against the backdrop of Freud's thoughts on the meting out of punishment by society.

By way of introduction, I suspect that three matters for me are homologously connected. First, I have a keener interest in examining society's desire to punish than in poring over the motivations of the criminal. Second, I find the recent inclination to attribute so much to countertransference far more notable than the expected lack of responsibility in the patient. I remember a case conference in which the therapist's failure to arrive for three sessions was attributed to the patient's so-called borderline aggression. Third, my interest is frequently more compelled by the band of brothers who so violently exhume Freud than with the actual life of this genius. I am reminded of two recent public lectures. In the first, Eysenck (1988) sought to blame Anna O's "tragic life" on the failure of Freud's treatment, paying no attention to the bit of reality that Freud, of course, never treated her and was only twenty-four years old when Breuer did. In the very same lecture, Eysenck reported that Little Hans remained a failure throughout life (he was, in fact, the well-published director of a major metropolitan music center), that the Wolf Man was seen by "Psychologist Obholzer" as still severely disturbed (Obholzer was a journalist who found a charming old gentleman nearing his death with some not insignificant degree of poise; see Obholzer 1982). In the second lecture, Roazen (1989) noted that there was something diabolical about Freud. When questioned, he responded that Freud was, after all, committed to his notion of a universal bisexual constitution! (The connection between a character flaw and a scientific postulate is difficult to follow logically.) With these in mind, I should like briefly to examine society's role in the meting out of punishment.

In listing fifty-five notes, comments, and objections about M'Naghten's Rules (the 1840s criminal insanity rule), Edward Glover (1951, 277) argues: "Criminal responsibility and the disposal of convicted criminals, although to this limited extent correlated in law, are nevertheless problems of an entirely distinct nature. The former is concerned with the diagnosis of the state of mind or body of offenders; the latter with their treatment." The words "responsible" and "responsibility," which both Glover and Dr. Solnit use, pose for me difficulties in and of themselves. When in our recent history, a president and one of his senior staff members admitted that they were ultimately responsible for confabulations presented to Congress, they were assuredly not indicating an *ability to respond correctively to their own actions* and certainly not that they were culpable or deserving of punishment. Nonetheless, Glover's distinction is helpful in that it separates out these two concerns.

Einstein, in his 1932 letter (reprinted with Freud's response in Freud and Einstein 1932) to Freud queried: "Is there any way of delivering mankind from the menace of war? The quest for international security involves the unconditional surrender by every nation, in a certain measure, of its liberty of action, its sovereignty that is to say, and it is clear beyond all doubt that no other road can lead to such security. Is it possible," he continues, "to control man's mental evolution so as to make him proof against the psychoses of hate and destructiveness?"

Freud's response, in contrast to Einstein's goad, is something akin to the distinction between what should be and what is, and is, I believe typical of Freud's view. Freud chooses to focus on the source of the inclination toward punishing the guilty. I present some selections from this answer.

It is a general principle, then, that conflicts of interest between men are settled by the use of violence . . . [and are] most completely achieved if the victor's violence eliminated his opponent permanently—that is to say, killed him. . . . Such was the original state of things: domination by whoever had the greater might—domination by brute violence or by violence supported by intellect. As we know, this regime was altered in the course of evolution. There was a path that led from violence to right or law. . . . Thus we see that right is the might of a community. It is still violence ready to be directed against any individual; it works by the same methods and follows the same purposes. The only real difference lies in the fact that what prevails is no longer the violence of an individual but that of a community. . . . Here, I believe, we already have all the essentials; violence overcome by the transference of power to a larger unity, which is held together by emotional ties between its members. What remains to be said is no more than an expansion and repetition of this." (Freud and Einstein 1932, 204–205)

Freud's view that justice is the violence of the community has particular relevance not only to the M'Naghten Rules and to its modifications in Durham and the Irresistible Impulse Test, but also to Dr. Solnit's requirement that one comes to hold oneself responsible for post-childhood behavior and development with only the child's responsibility for his actions. On this matter, by the way, I cannot fully agree with Dr. Solnit. *Anyone who murders is quite guilty of murder.* How we as a society choose to deal with those whose failure to recognize fully the subjectivity and intrinsic worth of another, whether in murder, larceny, or destruction of another person's property, is a different matter and relates more closely to our cultural narcissism than to an Aquinian notion of Natural Law or Natural Justice. I am reminded, with respect to the functionings of this cultural narcissism, of the recent outburst of rage against Saddam Hussein for failing to release the *women and children.* Ignoring, for the moment, the biological underpinnings that may have once contributed to the need to protect the women and children in order to promote population growth, our culture is clearly more willing to sacrifice males to bloodlusts and less willing to do so with women and children. This, however, should not be attributed to intrinsic qualities of the protected group in distinction from the sacrificial group, but rather to the culture's unwillingness to see itself as responsible for punishment or death in these groups. In the same fashion, it is not relevant to discuss criminal insanity pleas except from the perspective of the culture's need, or willingness to suspend its need, for retribution. Anyone who murders is quite guilty of murder. M'Naghten, the Irresistible Impulse Test, clemency, and children's courts are some indication of an incipient containment of societal bloodlust, of an awakening charity.

The M'Naghten Rule reads: ". . . to establish a defence on the grounds of insanity, it must be clearly proved that at the time of committing the act, the accused was labouring under such a defect of reason, from disease of the mind, as not to know the nature and quality of the act he was doing; or if he did know it, that he did not know he was doing what is wrong." I wonder how Freud, had he been a jurist, would have modified these rules that hide the true intent of judicial punishment, retribution. In talking of Dostoevsky's sympathy for the criminal (Freud 1927), which I suggest must be a near kin of our clemencies and special treatment of the weak, insane, and ill, Freud argues that "it is not just kindly pity, it is identification on the basis of a similar murderous impulse—in fact, a slightly displaced narcissism" (p. 190). Freud then adds parenthetically: "In saying this we are not disputing the ethical value of this kindness" (p. 190).

Before Freud, society—civilized society—may well have been satisfied by its comely explanations for the manner in which it punished its exceptions, its discontents. Society could cite the need for deterrence of would-be offenders and the need for justice to maintain law and order. Freud, however, has taught us that civilized human beings continue to equate "foreigner and enemy" (Freud 1915b, 277), that criminality or the failure to relinquish our supreme right to instinctual gratification at any cost will not soon, if ever, disappear, and that public executions are not staged to demonstrate the objective fairness of any Natural Law.

References

Eissler, K. R. 1975. The fall of man. *Psychoanalytic Study of the Child* 30:589–644.

Erikson, E. 1962. Reality and actuality. *Journal of the American Psychoanalytic Association* 10:451–474.

Eysenck, H. 1988. Fritz Nova Lecture delivered at Villanova University, Villanova, Pennsylvania, 10 November 1988.

Feldman, H. 1972. A psychoanalytic addition to human nature. *Psychoanalytic Review* 61:133–139.

Freud, S. 1894. The neuro-psychoses of defence. *S.E..* 3:41–61.

———. 1896. Further remarks on the neuro-psychoses of defence. *S.E.* 3:162–189.

———. 1915a. The unconscious. *S.E.* 14:159–204.

———. 1915b. Thoughts for the times on war and death. *S.E.* 14:273–300.

———. 1917. Introductory lectures on psychoanalysis. *S.E.* 16.

———. 1927. Dostoevsky and parricide. *S.E.* 21:173–194.

Freud, S., and Einstein, A. 1932. Why war? *S.E.* 22:199–210.

Ginzburg, L. 1920. *The Legends of the Jews.* 7 vols. Philadelphia: Jewish Publication Society.

Glover, E. 1951. Notes on the M'Naghten Rules. *British Journal of Delinquency* 1:276–282.

Kris, E. 1954. *The Origins of Psychoanalysis.* New York: Basic Books.

Obholzer, K. 1982. *The Wolf Man: Conversations with Freud's Patient Sixty Years Later.* New York: Continuum Publishing.

Roazen, P. 1989. The influence of Freud on social and political thought. Lecture at Temple University, Philadelphia, 28 September 1989.

7

An Interpretation of Four of Freud's Letters

K. R. Eissler

The psychologist-historian interested in the advance of science and its application is for obvious reasons often moved to examine failures in the course of a scholar's career; errors and faults are more effective in stimulating the quest for motives and causes than the successful completion of a project. Sometimes, however, psychologist-historians' assessments of what constitutes "failure," particularly when based on "common-sense" judgments, may lack objectivity. Recently, some investigators have centered on the question of why Freud abandoned the seduction theory. Since they deny that the seduction theory was false, they have groped for personal motives. They have made it appear as though Freud held a great truth in his hands but let it slip away for subjective,

This is an expanded version of a paper published by the National Psychological Association for Psychoanalysis, Inc. in *The Psychoanalytic Review* (vol. 78, pp. 1–35, 1991) entitled "Common Sense, Documentation, and the Method of Unrestricted Exegesis: Their Value and Limitations Examined in Four Letters by Freud." Reprinted by permission.

reprehensible reasons. Almost all such psychologist-historians did not consult relevant documents[1] in order to test their hunches but relied mainly on common sense.[2]

Recourse to common-sense judgments derives from the desire to save time and thought. They are necessary in most situations for survival and at the same time a frequent cause of derailments. It is a sign of wisdom to know when common sense can be relied on and when it invites disaster. Fitting into traditional views, the common-sense judgment invites approval and agreement. Thus common sense takes it for granted that day is light and night is dark. Yet the difference in light from day to night has prompted physicists to propose mutually contradictory theories in order to solve this seemingly simplest of all problems (Harrison 1984). Millions of people have idled away hours on the beach, but only Einstein wondered about the conspicuously different physical properties of dry, moist, and wet sand. To everyone else the differences were a matter of common sense.

The dictates of common sense change from one historical period to another, sometimes even from decade to decade. Throughout the medieval centuries, many regarded the existence of witches, witchcraft, and the devil as a matter of common sense. Thus the common-sense dictates of one period may be laughable or even appear, to those who live in later times, immoral and deserving of radical rejection and punishment. Common-sense judgments not only reveal the spirit of historical periods; more frequently than not, they divulge the personality of the person who voices them; that is to say, in addition to the common sense that dominates the majority within a society, there probably are variant types of common sense specific to class membership, social subgroups, and character types. A career-oriented mind, driven primarily by ambition and eager to receive popular approval, would take it for granted that Freud, fearful lest he lose out in the promotional game customary in academic institutions, would be quick to drop a theory that had made him unpopular in those circles. The common sense of a money-minded person, on the other hand, would be inclined to assume that Freud was eager to enlarge his practice and therefore was mindful of his standing with colleagues who might refer patients to him. The politically progressive mind, enthusiastic about social reforms and seeing in the seduction theory a criticism of society, would respond to the abandonment of that theory as a sign of the weakening of Freud's desire to reform society and suspect Freud of being a deserter, a turncoat who left a good cause for personal advantage.

Knowing of the inescapability and ubiquity of prejudice and bias, historians and other investigators try to combat their effects by careful study of documents. To give an example, what might common sense say to a remark Freud made in his letter to Fliess (Freud 1985) of 21 September 1897: "For certain I shall not speak about it [his error in putting forward the seduction-father theories] in Dan and not talk about it in Askelon, in the country of the Philistine"?[3] In this way Freud let his friend know that his confession of error was confidential and that for the time being he did not want the public to know of it.[4] The common-sense psychologist-biographer would perhaps pass this sentence by, ignoring the occasion for trying the establish its hidden meaning. Yet it is a pivotal and surprising statement that is all the more deserving of attention because it contains an error.

Freud referred here to II Samuel 1:20, where it says: "Tell it not in Gath, publish it not in the streets of Askelon." Why did he confuse Gath and Dan? Seventeen years earlier (23 July 1880), in a letter to a friend, he had quoted the passage correctly: "Do not speak of it in Askelon, do not announce it in the streets of Gath."[5] Furthermore, why did he quote the passage at all in that letter to Fliess? Dan, the city to which Freud erroneously referred, evokes tragic imagery. The children of Dan (one of the twelve tribes) "came into Laish, unto a people that were at quiet and secure; and they smote them with the edge of the sword and burnt the city with fire. And there was no deliverer because it was far from Zidon, and they had no business with any man. . . . And they built a city, and dwelt therein. And they called the name of the city Dan" (Judges 18:27–29). It is mentioned several times in the Bible in the context of defining the boundaries of a region: "from Dan to Beersheba." Gath and Askelon were the citadels of power of the Philistines, Israel's arch enemies, whereas Dan and Beersheba were names of localities associated with national catastrophes. According to Judges 20:1, the children of Israel "went out and the congregation was gathered together as one man, from Dan even to Beersheba," initiating events that led to the fratricidal slaughter of forty thousand Israelites and the desolation of the tribe of Benjamin. At the command of the Lord, David requested that "all the tribes of Israel, from Dan even to Beersheba" were to be numbered, which was a sin and led to a pestilence and the death of seventy thousand men "from Dan even to Beersheba" (II Samuel 24:15).

But what is the context in the Bible in which the Gath-Askelon statement occurs? In the battle against the Philistines, Saul the King lost his life at Mount Gilboa. In this moment of national calamity and humiliation, when his grieving heart was further torn by the irredeemable loss of his closest friend, Jonathan, Saul's son, who fell in the same battle, David pleaded for secrecy "lest the daughters of the Philistines rejoice, lest the daughters of the uncircumcised triumph." News of the national defeat should not be broadcast because it would give comfort and encouragement to the daughters of the enemy.

From this imagery hidden in Freud's simple quotation, one may infer that his perception of the basic flaw in the theory evoked a feeling of deep shame, disproving his boastful, thrice-repeated statements in his letter to Fliess that he was cheerful and in good spirits.[6] By not taking an analogy for granted, by not assigning to it the meaning of a mere stylistic curlicue, but by digging to the bottom of its possible meaning and scrutinizing the frame in which it originally appeared, an emotion is bared that had been denied *expressis verbis* by the initiator of the metaphor. The activation of that emotion can now be claimed with certainty.

The biblical quotation conspicuously refers to the triumph of the "uncircumcised," and circumcision in Vienna was at that time restricted to Jews. It was the last remaining visible "stigma" that differentiated assimilated Jews from the gentile community. Freud's fear might have been that some of his Christian colleagues would feel triumphant about the defeat of the Jewish boy or worse, Jew boy, who had come from an obscure provincial town and had had the temerity to challenge and provoke the medical hierarchy of Vienna by boasting that he had discovered a great truth, of the same order of importance as the Caput Nili, with "absolute certainty" (*absolute Sicherheit*), and that his findings were "self-evident" (*selbstverständlich*) and "clear like sunlight" (*sonnenklar*) (1896c). Such expressions are rarely heard in scientific discourse, and their use by Freud in reference to his own work is not to be found elsewhere in his writings.

The Gath-Askelon imagery cannot, indeed, be taken seriously enough. Hypnosis and cocaine had been defeats, but now a first-rate catastrophe had overtaken Freud. Would he ever be able to recover? From now on, whenever he appeared in public to present his findings, one of the Philistines would be entitled to get up and say, "Prove it. Once you said you saw the source of the Nile with your own eyes, and it was braggadocio. Why should we trust your sight this time?" Freud should have been apprehensive lest he had maneuvered himself into a position in which he had muzzled himself and lost the right to speak out ever again in professional gatherings. There was one redeeming feature, such as it may have been: he had not spoken publicly of his theory that the fathers of his female patients had been perverts, which he had communicated on a number of occasions to his friend. No one, of course, knew what Freud had written to Fliess.

It is understandable by mere empathy that the Gath-Askelon imagery came to Freud's mind in connection with the defeat of the seduction theory, which he loved as much as David loved Jonathan. But nothing in Freud's tie to it contains a hint of why the Gath-Dan error occurred. Dan and Gath are, as I noted, associated with egregious calamities, and yet there was one decisive difference between them. The catastrophes that occurred when the Benjamites were defeated and that followed the numbering were pure waste: they did not lead to advancement of any sort. Saul's defeat, however, initiated David's rise to kingship and a glorious chapter in the history of the Israelites. Hence, the error may clarify a doubt to which Freud alluded at another place, namely, as to whether he had reached a point of no return or whether he could expect victories like David's. In other words, his hope for a turning point was confronted by the dismal prospect of never making a lasting discovery in the future.

In 1897, when he discovered that his "neurotica" were wrong, Freud would have been less distressed if he had limited himself in the year before to the publication of the two papers he had finished at the beginning of the year (1896a, 1896b) and not exposed himself by specifically lecturing to the profession of his hometown. After all, his conscious motive and proximate purpose for publishing this lecture (1896c) were not aboveboard. "In defiance of my colleagues," he wrote Fliess on the day it appeared in print (30 May 1896), "I have put into writing in detail . . . my address about aetiology of hysteria." Sometimes defiance backfires on the defiant.

In discussing Freud's use of the Dan-Askelon imagery, by following what may be called the principle of unrestricted exegesis, I slipped without fanfare into psychoanalytic common sense—that is, a set of working hypotheses which initially may have been defined relatively carefully and may have been subjected to critical discussion but in due course came to be taken for granted by a group marked off by its special professional and scientific goals and shared methodology (cf. Thomas Kuhn). The principle of unrestricted exegesis states that the content of an analogy may be interpreted ad infinitum in all possible directions: literal, literary, personal, historical, and symbolic; that is, it may be looked upon as a day residue, as a derivative of a repressed impulse, as a biographical element, as a referent to a historical event, or as if it were part of a legend, fairy tale, or an archaic symbol derived from any area of culture, religion, art, and what not. I have taken the category of analogy as the most suitable example for a discussion of unrestricted exegesis, but this principle extends to any element that is the carrier of significant unconscious meanings.

The application of unrestricted exegesis has gone hand in hand with a disregard of the usual constraints imposed by the logic of time. That is, the biographical methodology of psychoanalysis has permitted a relaxation of the customary research conventions, insofar as biographical episodes and elements have been ordered and grouped without regard to their sequences and proximity in time; they have been brought into meaningful contexts even when separated by decades. This has been done in conformity with observations based on dream interpretation and the recognition of the timelessness, perhaps even atemporality, of the unconscious (cf. Freud 1915e, 187). It is a peculiar paradox: to understand the mind's workings without recourse to temporal categories is virtually inconceivable, and yet psychoanalysis is forced to abrogate time in certain areas if it wants to grasp the deepest of the human; it has to thrust forth to levels that are beyond any infiltration of the temporal dimension. There is, thus, in psychoanalysis a kind of "amorality" with regard to time comparable to what can be observed in children who arbitrarily confuse yesterday and tomorrow. This amorality stands in strict contrast to the great emphasis on exactness in the psychoanalytic reconstruction of a subject's past. There it makes an essential difference whether an event took place a year, a month, a week, or sometimes even a day earlier or later. Amorality and great precision in time relations are both significant of psychoanalysis.

It is well known that once a new science has demonstrated its value and has earned a following, it brings forth a stream of surprising discoveries. Such discoveries gradually give birth to the rules, expectations, thought patterns, and habitual inferences which in turn come to be taken for granted and then compose a new "common sense," as indicated above. Psychoanalysis is, by and large, in that phase, but the common sense of academic psychology and everyday reasoning has not diminished its hold on Western thinking. This results in the curious situation in which I am combatting the common sense of some Freud critics by applying working hypotheses that some might regard as reflecting or incorporating a new common sense. In the following pages, by "common sense" I mean nonanalytic common sense. If one tries to uncrate some of Freud's mental processes during that fateful period when he had to give up believing his "neurotica," one certainly cannot depend on common sense. The biographer of that period will examine the documents over and over again, searching for idiosyncratic elements.[7]

The traditional psychologist is satisfied when he has identified motives that are to be expected in the average instance. To be sure, most people seek to profess attitudes and opinions in keeping with others of their community. What is original, personal, and individual is more frequently than not devoured by the unconscious without seeing daylight. In proposing that Freud renounced the seduction theory in order to return to the good graces of his colleagues,

Masson (1984) was, as I have argued, mistaken; but he was right in his underlying common-sense premise, in that many, perhaps even most, researchers would have dropped a theory that had aroused opposition of the intensity to which Freud seemed to have been subjected on the occasion of his lecture in 1896. But how many would have quoted II Samuel 1:20, and how many would have kept it secret for eight years that they were no longer asserting the offensive theory?

To return to unrestricted exegesis, for the analyst its application makes the quotation in its original, complete, biblical form an exciting and promising cue that opens up an area without defined borders. Just as the dream, according to Freud, is determined by an indefinite number of elements and is the carrier of memories, feelings, fantasies, impulses, bodily sensations, and what not, so, too, a turn so surprising as the Gath-Askelon allusion can hardly be interpreted so extensively as to make one certain of having reached the limits of interpretive possibilities; a new document, a new literary source, even the interpreter's sudden thought or fancy, may add new meanings. The relative poverty and monotony of the observations possible within the framework of the traditional psychologist, should he become interested in the motives and other antecedent elements related to Freud's Bible quotation, are replaced by a potential wealth of ideas and possibilities. Of course there is the danger of over- and misinterpretation. Even if there should be, let us hope, allusions, connotations, and innuendos at hand that might be used as safeguards, or that might help to find the way back to the right path, the method of unrestricted exegesis as used in psychoanalytic research, despite, or even because of, its enormously productive potential, needs a methodology safeguarding against over- and faulty interpretation. Indeed, here is an area of weakness in the field of applied psychoanalysis.

The results of unrestricted exegesis have, of course, the standing of hypotheses, but in most instances they will be taken as the final results of psychoanalytic ratiocination. In reference to Freud's Dan-Gath error, a critic may demand proof that Freud knew the Bible to the extent that the inferences I have presented would appear to presuppose. According to the principle of unrestricted exegesis, however, such a proof would not be required. Evidently Dan had become a meaningful element or it could not have appeared in the wrong context. The reconstruction I added does not go beyond what an analyst is accustomed to doing in the clinical practice of dream interpretation. Once something is in the unconscious it is a potation brewing in a cauldron. The proposition that the error mirrors a specific aspect of Freud's reaction to his discovery of the intrinsic error in his esteemed theory, namely, simultaneous hope and desolation, is a hypothesis and far removed from any rigorous statement of fact, but good enough to be considered.

The Gath-Askelon simile proves that Freud was in love with the seduction-father theory. He compared its loss to David's loss of his dearest friend. How much Freud loved the theory can be seen from the quickness with which he responded to a sign (Emma Eckstein's premature and evidently misleading statement that she had confirmed it) that it may have after all been correct. If Masson's interpretation conformed to fact, Freud should have regretted the revival of that possibility, for it would force him to slide back into his colleagues' disdain. To be sure, Freud was not surrounded by nothing but ruins: "In this collapse of all values the psychological alone remained untouched," he reported proudly. "The dream stands here quite secure, and the beginnings of my metapsychological work have nothing but gained in appreciation. A pity that one cannot live, for example, from the interpretation of dreams" (21 September 1897).

And—it must further be asked—what would the traditional psychologist make of Freud's ostensible error, when, in a series of letters to Fliess beginning 6 December 1896, he converted an almost clear-cut "brother theory" (among twelve culprits seven brothers had seduced their sisters) into a "father theory"? This derailment has prompted little interest. Freud also let Hamlet kill Laertes instead of Polonius. He tried to exemplify Hamlet's rashness and impetuosity but writes as if he had killed the son (15 October 1897), that is to say, he was as rash as Hamlet when as a child he killed off the infant brother. Freud's guilt about his infant brother's death was probably operative throughout his life.[8] This *lapsus calami* becomes the key to an understanding of a covert problem. The Polonius-Laertes confusion reveals personal guilt. It says that the son was the guilty party, not the father (in the form of the senile Polonius): it is the brother who deserves punishment. It also should not be forgotten that Hamlet brought calamity on a sister-figure, and Laertes sought revenge for this crime.

I do not follow this path to its end here but turn to another quotation in the letter of 21 September 1897 that embodies a different aspect of Freud's identification with Hamlet and possibly comprises a distinct, important biographical strand. When announcing the discovery of his error to Fliess in September 1897, Freud was in doubt as to how to interpret it. Were the doubts in his old theory the result of weakness, signs of fatigue, or should he have been proud that he had enough critical acumen to revise a theory to which he had committed himself? As noted above, he asked, was "this doubt only an episode in the progression toward further insights?" He modified Hamlet's words "the readiness is all" (which he quoted in English) to *"Heiter sein ist alles." Heiter* is difficult to translate. It is an amalgam of "cheerful," "buoyant," "carefree," that is, "endowed with a happy disposition free of passions."[9] What is the background of Freud's changing Shakespeare's "The readiness is all" (Hamlet, V/2, 1.234) to "to be *heiter* is all"?

When Osric, a symbol of the messenger of death in a satirized form, brings the king's request that he engage in a duel with Laertes, Hamlet accepts it. But Hamlet voices forebodings "as perhaps would trouble a woman," and Horatio offers to accommodate his lord and "forestall their [the court's] repair hither and say you are not fit." Hamlet rejoins: "Not a whit, we defy augury: there is special providence in the fall of a sparrow. If it be now, 'tis not to come; if it be not to come, it will be now; if it be not now, yet it will come; the readiness is all." This is a statement of awe-inspiring depth and breadth: a climax in itself in that it vanquishes time by almost grinding it to dust in three magnificent contradictions that defy logic and convey a world of archaic beauty and meaning. Hamlet has freed himself of impulses of revenge; he has accepted the mission with which his father has burdened him; his rage at Claudius's crimes has vanished. These three conditions are mutually contradictory, as are his three statements about time; they denote a mind that at last has reached a point of supreme tolerance toward a world which, in view of all its egregious deficiencies, is in the end undeserving of it. He has learned to accept it as is. He is temporarily conflict-free. Freud could have reproached Brücke, as we will see, for letting him publish prematurely, his father for being a poor provider and burdening him with adult responsibilities before he was mature enough to carry them out ("The worries that have deprived me of my youth," he wrote in the same letter), and Fliess for not warning him against the trap of the seduction-father theory. But he had dropped aggression (had that perhaps facilitated his divesting himself of the father theory?) and was "ready" to accept whatever his future might harbor.[10]

Freud's conjuring up, in that moment, Hamlet on his way to the fatal duel is suggestive of all kinds of possibilities. The context in which Freud quoted Hamlet contains basic contradictions no less than the quotation itself. Special providence makes readiness unnecessary, perhaps even impossible, and Freud, acknowledging his failure and the impossibility of discovering the etiology of the psychoneuroses, had no reason to feel confident about the future. He did not suspect, when he put his trust in Providence, that he would be the one to make a momentous step forward in liberating mankind from the shackles of concepts of that kind. Did not Freud by virtue of psychoanalysis reveal Providence to be the voice of the unconscious? Personal mishaps, adversities, sicknesses that were upheld as signs and illustrations of Providence were increasingly unmasked as the inadvertent arrangements of the sufferer's unconscious. Here is a discovery that destroys the awesome implications of fate and destiny. Furthermore, in Hamlet's statement of serenity, which was not *heiter* at all, about what will come to pass and what will not, one may discover the ambience of the future psychoanalytic situation of free association, in which the subject is supposed to bow to whatever his unconscious will dredge up on the spur of the moment, in which the subject faces uncertainty as to whether the anticipated will or will not make its appearance in his mind, and in which the mind faces an unstructured moment in which past, present, and future cross or conjoin, amalgamate, or annul each other. Hamlet preserved a core of tranquility despite the prospect of turmoil and perturbation; Freud pretended to do the same when he wrote Fliess in September; and as a matter of fact, he would later educate those who subjected themselves to his analysis to preserve that core in the same way. But this was still quite far off in September 1897.

The next question concerns the source of the *Heiterkeit* which was to replace Hamlet's readiness. Wilhelm Knöpfmacher[11] (1853–1937) told his son that Freud once compared himself to the young man in "The Veiled Image at Sais," a famous epic poem by Schiller (Knöpfmacher 1970, 60) in which an Egyptian youth "was driven by the hot thirst for knowledge to Sais in order to learn" the priests' secret wisdom. He advanced with speed; learning enthralled him. "What do I have if I do not have everything?" he said. "Is your Faith only a sum" of more and less? he asked. "Is truth not unique and indivisible?" This is reminiscent of the young Freud in his restless striving to understand man and the world. The young Egyptian of Schiller's poem once saw an image of giant size behind the veil of which, his priest-teacher told him, was hidden the truth. The neophyte complained that the truth which he came to Sais to obtain was withheld from him. The priest divulged the Goddess's pronouncement: "No mortal [dare] move the veil before I myself lift it." Yet the young man slunk at night into the temple and lifted the veil. He was found pale and unconscious the following day, prostrate in front of Isis's simulacrum. What he had seen his tongue never revealed. Forever gone was his life's *Heiterkeit*.

And now we know why "readiness" in the Hamlet quotation was altered to *heiter*. For Freud was not ready as Hamlet was. Freud had had enough of the continuous chain of disappointments. That little detail, of replacing "readiness" by "*Heiterkeit*," which looks like an inconsequential flourish, adds renewed evidence that those who attribute to Freud all kinds of selfish reasons for dropping the seduction theory are wrong and lack understanding of what goes on in the mind of a creative giant. Freud, like his Egyptian forebear, was heartbroken. He certainly did not want this to be revealed to his friend; perhaps he even succeeded in concealing it to a large degree from himself. Saul's defeat and suicide and Jonathan's death and the outcry for *Heiterkeit*—these allusions strike tragic chords. After all, Freud had acted like his Egyptian forebear and attended schools of higher learning; he had chosen outstanding teachers and been the faithful pupil of great contemporary scholars; and after the proper time of apprenticeship had elapsed, he had tried to use his own good luck and lift the Goddess's veil; indeed, Isis gave him the illusion of descrying the long-sought Caput Nili. The Goddess had deceived him by luring him along to let him be caught in an invisible trap. The only advice the stricken hero in the poem gave an interrogator was: Woe to him who advances through guilt to truth; it will never be enjoyable to him. Freud might have offered the same counsel. Did he not write Fliess that the origin of neurosis could not be uncovered? Was the Caput Nili not covered by forbidding mist? The Goddess would never unveil her face; therefore, he was not ready for new adventures of exploration. He asked only to be left undisturbed and feel *heiter*, the feeling which the Egyptian novice had lost forever. The experience of this feeling, Freud hoped, would protect him against the collapse which the other, according to Schiller, had irremediably suffered. Only an unbounded effort could generate *Heiterkeit* in Freud on that fateful 21 September 1897.

I should rejoice if it could be demonstrated that unrestricted exegesis can bring light into all recesses of biographical darkness. However, in Freud's correspondence one finds instances that seem to demonstrate that even a liberal application of unrestricted exegesis does not always lead to enlightenment. Freud's letter of 6 August 1878 to his friend Wilhelm Knöpfmacher contains such instances, puzzling key issues to which biographers have given insufficient attention.[12] To my ear the letter sounds as if Freud had been in a mildly euphoric mood when he wrote it. The associations are loosened, the humor mildly exaggerated and forced, alternating between self-elevation and self-degradation. Freud was then twenty-two years old. He had borrowed money from his friend, who was three years older than he. It was, as Freud wrote, returned "in haste" because "Vile base Mammon melts away in so alarming a way in my hands that, in an honest man's fear lest he offend obligations I wanted to deliver [*literally,* rescue] my treasure into your hands." The well-known "stone" (as the German vernacular has it) fell from his heart. If there is a God, Freud wrote, he will repay one-thousandfold, and if not, there will be a man who will not forget and have one more reason to keep on loving his friend. "I transmit also my collected works" (1877a, 1877b), he continued, "not my complete ones as I have reason to conjecture for I am just now waiting for the galley proof of a third one [1878a], and a fourth and fifth announce themselves to my presentient soul[13] which [is] frightened by it like Macbeth in view of the ghosts of the English kings." " 'It will take no end, I fear, until the last day,' " Freud added, referring to the scene in Shakespeare's tragedy in which Macbeth encounters the future kings of England. This strange, self-mocking remark is followed by another no less odd: He has moved into another laboratory, he wrote, where "[I] prepare myself for my real profession, to flay animals or torment humans," which is a slightly faulty quotation from a comical book for children, *Max und Moritz* by Wilhelm Busch (1832–1908), about the pranks of two delinquent latency youngsters. But first to Shakespeare.

"It will take no end, I fear, until the Last Judgment"[14] is an English rendering of the German translation that was current at that time of Shakespeare's "What, will the line stretch out to th' crack of doom?" (*Macbeth* IV/1, l. 117), which refers to Macbeth's confrontation with the ghosts of the future kings who will not be the product of his loins. Freud's allusion sounds like self-mockery, for publications on the central nervous system would not bear comparison to kings, of whatever domain. The collected works were two papers that had been published (1877a, 1877b); the galleys of a third (1878a) were on their way. They amounted to a true triumph for the twenty-two-year-old tyro who held no academic position. It is possible that unconsciously he had formed a megalomanic self-fantasy that may have resulted in a minor euphoria; some may think that he had the right to feel that way about himself. Thus, one may dismiss the Macbeth allusion as no more than a student's banter, a beginner's overvaluation of his first steps in the field then called natural philosophy. Although this common-sense inference may to a certain extent have its validity, it would be a mistake to let the matter rest there, forgoing the opportunity to explore the depths to which the tragic aspect may lead that Freud conjured up with the Shakespeare quotation.

It is uncanny to ponder that the young student setting out on his scientific trek identified with a figure who killed a king and was a murderer of children. The ominous portent of that identification must by no means be underrated. Thirty-two years later (6 March

1910), in a communication to his friend the Reverend Pfister (1873–1956), one reencounters an allusion to an identification with Macbeth—this time, of a different order, since it is a desirable one: "I have one quite secret prayer, that I may be spared any wasting away and crippling of my ability to work because of physical deterioration. In the words of King Macbeth, let us die in harness" (Freud, 1963a). This echoed Shakespeare's line, "Blow wind, come, wrack, / At least we'll die with harness on our back" (*Macbeth* V/5, ll. 51–52).[15]

Thus, both while looking into the future as a young man and while contemplating the end of life at the peak of maturity, Freud spoke with Macbeth's voice. Freud's closeness to Macbeth in his prediction of a third, a fourth, a fifth publication is striking, for it repeats almost word for word the latter's horror-stricken outcry: "A third . . . a fourth . . . a seventh." Macbeth was forced to acknowledge that his dearest wishes will be foiled: not his own, but his adversaries' progeny would reign; his crimes had been fruitless. In order to fulfill his burning ambitions, in order to realize a mission into which he was deceptively lured by the world yonder, he had loaded his conscience with devastating guilt, which is, one may say, man's greatest possible sacrifice; but all for naught: he failed. The *tertium comparationis* in the life of the young Freud is by no means obvious. Why should a stigma of guilt—ostensibly of crushing intensity—be attached to the forthcoming papers, which if the analogy is taken literally, would not even have been his? Here the commentator would have the right to lay down his arms.

But one may ask, did Macbeth and Freud, after all, have a feature in common? Both were chosen. Macbeth was chosen by three sisters of destiny for a future that clashed with all law and order. Freud, too, was tied to fate by strong bonds. As a Jew he was, according to the Old Testament, one of the children chosen by Jehovah. A second sense in which he was chosen was an early tie to the biblical Joseph through an identification (Shengold 1971) that would later make him, too, a famous interpreter of dreams. The recognition of the identity of his family position with Joseph's was virtually inescapable since both his spiritual ancestor and he shared a remarkable number of features. Both were the eldest sons in a second marriage; their mothers were the favorite wives, their fathers' name was Jacob, and they were their favorite sons. The third instance of Freud's being chosen was more recent: he was selected by his admired and feared teacher, Ernst Brücke (1819–1892), a suitable modern substitute for Jehovah, to do research, an honor even greater than the privilege of being the first in the family to attend a Christian institution of higher learning.

The principle of unrestricted exegesis thus would lead to the equivalence of the three witches who chose Macbeth and the three forces, Jehovah, Jacob Freud, and Professor Brücke. In their first meeting, the sisters of destiny implanted the anticipation of a glorious future in Macbeth. Freud knew about Macbeth's final catastrophe; did he fear lest fate had devised for him, too, a wretched ending?

The quotation that followed the allusion to Macbeth in Freud's letter to Knöpfmacher, the shift from Shakespeare to Wilhelm Busch, the arch-humorist known to every German-speaking person, was truly a leap *du sublime au ridicule.* Freud had changed laboratories during the summer; as we have seen, he wrote, "I prepare myself [at the new laboratory] for my real profession, to flay animals or torment humans," and he followed this with the comment "and I decide [myself] more and more for the first term of the alternative" (Freud 1960a). In the laboratory of the Institute for General and Experimental Pathology directed by Professor Salomon Stricker (1834–1898), Freud was not assigned to conduct histological research, as in Brückes laboratory, but rather had to conduct experiments with live animals (Jones 1953–1957, 1:54); thus the reference to "flaying animals." "To flay animals or torment humans" was, as noted, an erroneous quotation, for Busch's text reads, "to tease people and torment animals." It is worth quoting the pertinent section from the preamble. Max and Moritz were boys

> Who instead of, through wise teaching
> Becoming devoted to good things
> Ofttimes laughed about them
> And in secret made fun of them.
> Yes, to do evil
> Yes, for that one is ready!
> To tease[16] people, to torment animals

To steal apples, pears, plums
This indeed is more agreeable
And also more convenient
Than to sit tight on a chair
In church or school
But woe, woe, woe!
When I look at the end
Oh, that was a ghastly thing
How it went with Max and Moritz.[17]

Their end is really worse than Macbeth's. They are ground up in a mill and eaten by barnyard fowl. Freud's distortion of sequence and content are quite remarkable. Again the future is viewed in dismal terms. Freud had an excellent memory and he had read the book, I am sure, as a child and knew it by heart, wherefore the error cannot be attributed to accident. It is not difficult to divine the proximate source of the allusion to flaying, namely, the afore-mentioned experiments in Stricker's laboratory that required vivi-section, a procedure that must have unnerved the sensitive young student. And why did he characterize medical practice as torment-ing patients? In contemplating the steps that brought him to medi-cine, he wrote, later, "I have never really been a doctor in the proper sense. . . . I have no knowledge of having had any craving in my early childhood to help suffering humanity. My innate sadistic disposition was not a very strong one" (1927a, 253).[18] The error Freud made when quoting Busch would, in contradiction to the just-cited statement, intimate that medical practice did, after all, contain a sadistic meaning and that therefore he shunned it. But perhaps more meaningful is the striking fact that the comical ver-sion with its thrice-repeated *Wehe, Wehe, Wehe* at the end epito-mizes the essence of the tragic mood that is pervasive in the Mac-beth ghost scene. This identity permits the assumption that not mere coincidence but a hidden feeling of despair regarding the future was at work in the selection of both quotations. In fact, as things turned out, the task to which Freud was assigned that sum-mer in Stricker's laboratory came to naught and he returned to Brücke.

The two analogies, Macbeth and Max and Moritz, are widely disparate, by virtue not only of the differences between their authors but also of their subject matters: one takes us to royalties, historical personages of great renown, the other, to the anonymous low class. The royalties appear in the context of collected works and galleys, and the anonymous pranksters in the setting of flaying animals. It would seem that working in neurohistology and publishing crystal-clear papers are vastly superior to experimental work with animals. Royalty and the mediocrity of the pranksters paralleled another extreme contrast, that of Brücke, the professor of physiology versus Salomon Stricker, under whose authority Freud worked when he wrote the letter.

I must interpolate here a remark about personalities who served as ideals in Freud's early life. His father, whom he loved, did not live up to the demands he expected to be fulfilled in a male ideal. Of the early leaders Carl Brühl, Carl Claus, Salomon Stricker, and Brücke, only the latter fulfilled them: he was perfect in Freud's eyes and continued to be so to the end. Brühl and Claus were surrounded by controversy (a description that I do not intend to document but ask the reader to accept), as was Stricker—the latter because he had been made chief of the Institute against the opposition of the faculty; it had been, in fact, only through the efforts of Carl von Rokitansky (1804–1878), the most famous medical authority at the University of Vienna at that time, that the resistance of some faculty members to Stricker's promotion to professor had been overcome. Stricker's inadequacy as an ideal authority might have been a potent factor in Freud's feeling degraded to the status of Max and Moritz while working in Stricker's laboratory. He spent six months in the Institute for General and Experimental Pathology, according to Stricker's report (1879a), but it is not known why he had temporarily shifted from Brücke's institute, to which he felt inordinately attached. The fact that Stricker was a Jew might have promised the absence of prejudice, but such was certainly not present at Brücke's esablishment, either. One may conjecture that Brücke's institute, because of its long history of accomplishment and its fame, appeared to offer no opportunity for quick advancement, whereas Stricker's institute, founded only five years earlier, in 1873, may have seemed to be a setting in which rapid promotion could be expected.

Be that as it may, Freud did not succeed with Stricker. In two reports (1879a, 1879b), one learns of the task at which Freud failed. It had to do with glands: how do they work? do they secrete or excrete? Tissue had to be cut from the area surrounding the eyes of frogs and dogs, and thus vivisection was one of the methods. Freud did not have a blood phobia, as some claim, but the ambience of Stricker's laboratory must have been repellent. The error of "flaying animals" almost proves it. One of Freud's preconscious thoughts may have been, 'If I go on at Stricker's I am not better than Max and Moritz, who had one goal and purpose only—how to make themselves nuisances to everyone on earth.' Since they were ultimately devoured by birds and the punishment fits the crime, one may infer that oral aggression was activated unconsciously in the student surrounded by suffering creatures that are taken apart while still alive, degraded to satisfy human curiosity.

This account may approximately suffice to explain Freud's choice of Busch's delinquent pranksters as symbolic equivalents of the climate prevailing at Stricker's institute, but what about the ghosts of English kings who were not Macbeth's progeny representing Freud's papers? An incident trivial to us but frightening to the student impressed him as though punishment for hubris was close at hand. Its source can be found in the very paper—Freud's third; triplets are frequent in this context—whose galleys he was awaiting as he wrote Knöpfmacher. In the fall of 1876 Brücke submitted a paper by the student to the Academy of Science; to approve a student's work for publication so early in his career is unusual. It was the second paper Freud had written but the first to be published over his name (Freud 1877a). Brücke had given him the task of investigating the histologic features of the spinal cord of a primitive fish, the larval form of the brook lamprey (cf. Freud 1897b, 288; Jones 1953–1957, 1:46–48).

The galleys Freud was expecting were of a paper (1878a) in which he reported his continuing research on the spinal cord of the same fish. In compiling an eighteen-page bibliography for that paper, he made a discovery that evidently distressed him inordinately since the fifth section of the paper starts ominously: "At this point I must accuse[19] myself of having falsely thought that I was the first one to describe—based on direct and certain observations—the origin of the posterior nerve roots." Only after the publication of the paper in which he had claimed originality did he find an abstract of a Russian paper by Kutschin.[20] From the illustrations in that author's original publication he discovered that his own discovery had already been made seventeen years earlier. "By way of apology I can only say that Kutschin's statements—perhaps because his pictures were not available to the German histologists—were quite generally overlooked" (Jones 1953–1957, 1:47). The occasion of that public self-accusation would thus appear to have been a trivial instance of a pardonable oversight that was not even deserving to be called negligence. The offense was that a beginner in the field had published a finding as a discovery, not knowing that the same finding had already been published, albeit in a foreign publication of whose language he was ignorant. Freud would have had all the more reason to hold himself blameless since his teacher Brücke had urged publication in spite of Freud's reluctance (cf. Jones 1953–1957, 1:47).

Yet minuscule as the student's "crime" was, it might have struck him as similar to Macbeth's. As the kings of England were revealed not to be Macbeth's progeny, so would the papers under his name be suspected of containing "plagiarism," even if that misdemeanor had not been intended and in fact had not occurred. Indeed, when an author publishes something as an original contribution, he can never be dead sure that someone will not call him a plagiarist. Freud's conscience must have been overly sensitive, at least by present-day standards. The unusual seriousness and sense of duty and obligation with which the young man went about his studies and research are unmistakable.

What was the probable unconscious meaning of Freud's general sense of culpability? The dismal gloominess of the Macbeth imagery that followed Freud into his adult years makes sense when Freud's free access to academic institutions is viewed historically. At present, it is perhaps difficult to imagine what it meant to Freud and his family that without fuss and fanfare, as though it were a routine matter, the adolescent registered as a regular student at the university. He was given stipends, and then it even happened that papers were published under his name. The youth's father had been born in a ghetto; he and his eldest son still had to apply for official permission to stay for any length of time in communities away from their birthplace. Freud's rise was one from slums to riches.

Indeed, it sounds like a fairy tale when one visualizes the father driving his cart over the miserable trek in order to eke out a halfway-bearable existence and the son's rise to world fame. Jews might have fared better in other cultures than the Austro-Hungarian monarchy, but the recognition accorded the young Freud's achievements was a new element for central and eastern European Jewry, and the youth knew that. In his unconscious imagination he must have felt like a lucky intruder, particularly since the father emphasized the difference between now and then (cf. 1900a, 197) and the academic environment tried to impress upon him over and over again that he should regard himself as belonging to an inferior race (cf. Freud 1925d). After all, if he had been born only a few years earlier, he would not have been given the opportunities that were offered now in almost unimaginable measure. At the same time he was made to feel that he was not welcome and still carried the inferior-race stigma. Like Macbeth, Freud raised himself to a station that was above his father's and the rest of his family's, and this may have resulted in a deep feeling of guilt, and certainly in a feeling of liability.

Twenty-five years after the humorous-gloomy letter containing the references to Macbeth and Max and Moritz, Freud stood on the Acropolis, an experience that was at the center of a later paper (1936a). Looking from his father's birthplace, Tysmenitza in Galicia, which Freud never saw, to the Acropolis, which the father never saw, one can see a breathtaking rise, and Freud, a dutiful son, was overwhelmed by a feeling of guilt and indebtedness. The inner convulsion must have been extraordinary, for he asked his bewildered brother, who was his traveling companion, whether it really was true that they were standing on the Acropolis (Jones 1953–1957, 2:24). Many a strain in the paper of 1936 points back to the letter of the twenty-two-year-old.

The doubt about "Shall I be able to fulfill my obligations?" was adumbrated in the pretended banter, *Wehe, Wehe, Wehe,* of the second quotation. For some young men it is a Promethean triumph to tower above and eclipse their progenitors. In Freud, Promethean impulses probably simmered, as they do in any youth, but were they activated during that period? The way he cited Macbeth in 1878 sounds as if he had been afraid of them. In 1910, when he was closer to victory than thirty-two years before, fear of hubris had not vanished. The Macbeth identification is still visible as a scar, but the initial fear-arousing aspect had been converted into a desirable one. As a student he feared lest he might be or become a Macbeth, whereas as a professor he wished to be like Macbeth and be subjected to the kind of death Macbeth had been privileged to suffer, a privilege cruel nature denied him.

On the other hand, the youth may have thought that the probable future, when viewed realistically, was too nice to be true, that the cornucopia of good things with which fate had showered him had to end in a cataclysm; such a train of thought would in turn add strength to a Macbeth identification. In connection with this possibility, I must point out that according to occasional remarks Freud made, he seemed to have had an apprehensive attitude toward psychoanalysis as well. There are faint signs that Freud did not at all times accept psychoanalysis as his own accomplishment, as his discovery. He felt that by unmerited good luck he had come across a treasure of which he was not the true owner, and which he therefore had to hand out to others. Did he not write (to Fliess) of the mind's undiscovered provinces, which he had been the first to enter, none of which would carry his name or obey his laws (7 May 1900, the day after his first birthday in the new century)? It is the imagery of a discovery like that of Columbus, which did not aggrandize the discoverer's wealth and power. Unmistakably, furthermore, it points back to Macbeth, who also was not permitted to govern provinces with his own laws. Psychoanalysis seemed to have meant to Freud something that was not primarily connected with him. Once he wrote (1918b, 96) "I regard it as greatly to the credit of psychoanalysis . . . ," seemingly denying that the merits of psychoanalysis would be his. After Abraham's death in 1925 he wrote to Jones that "the loss was irreplaceable" (30 December), and he continued, "but what concerns [our] endeavors no one is allowed to be irreplaceable. . . . [T]he work must be continued compared with whose magnitude we all taken together are small." Clearly, psychoanalysis was viewed and experienced on that and other occasions as an awe-inspiring structure existing independently and outside of him; past, present, and future psychoanalysis is greater than he and all other psychoanalysts.

Only toward the end of his life, when Freud touched upon the smallness and frailty and the uncertain prognosis of his accomplishment, did he acknowledge a possessive sentiment: "More than a small fragment of truth one has not puzzled out. The proximate future looks gloomy also for my psychoanalysis" (to Stefan Zweig, 17 October 1937). The "my" sounds affectionate, but it is striking that it occurs in a context in which negative elements are enumerated.

One may, on the other hand, accord Freud's communication to his friend of 1878 a different valence and attribute to it a function not commonly thought to pertain to a letter. Freud was accustomed to being his parents' and sisters' favorite. But incidentally to studies and research he outgrew the comfort of closeness. He probably felt that his life with his family was no longer the center of his existence, that this center had moved away from the hearth. This was a knotty problem leading to the question: "Will I also be a favorite out there in the world of strangers?" Freud was in his tenth semester at that time and was to have graduated soon thereafter.[21] The letter contains an inner logical scheme. As noted, he starts with an endorsement of his good name by paying a debt sooner than his creditor requested. Speed protected him against dissipating the loan. Did this affirmation contrast with the father's perpetual financial embarrassment? He cannot reciprocate his benefactor with equal substantiality but with affection and the certainty that God's justice will reward his friend's good deed. The next element in the scheme asserts the value of his present existence in the form of two published papers and the announcement of a third. In that moment he sees himself standing at a watershed. The future, always unknown, may be cataclysmic. His situation of 1878 prompted, as the only security measure, his conjuring up (when he was still protected by family closeness), in a magical ritual, a future in which he would be exposed to the worst that could happen to him. That worst was the ignominy of a misappropriated kingship or of being a juvenile prankster, a good-for-nothing. Here the young Freud went through the symbolism of a rite of passage. The immediate reality situation seems to have been unfavorable.

Stricker had given him an assignment he was unable to live up to, and the situation was aggravated by his exposure to vivisection. His inclination to choose as a future profession "to flay animals" did not give rise to an enjoyable prospect. On the other hand, even his trusted ideal, Brücke, had misled him and exposed him to the necessity of publicly apologizing for misbehavior. By making himself for a moment the object of extreme calamities, Freud tried to bring about a benign future, as a rite of passage is supposed to do.

Freud experienced himself sometimes as a victim of adversities, but contrary to Macbeth, who was felled by them, Freud profited from them. The great trauma caused by paternal failure, which led him to lose the exhilarating, joyful ambience of country life at the age of three, brought him to Vienna. Had the father succeeded in gaining a substantial livelihood in Freud's provincial birthplace, Freud would have remained for many years to come in a culturally degraded environment. If there had been a vacancy in Brücke's institute and Freud could have continued to explore the histology of the nervous system, which had become almost an addicting passion, he certainly would have never acquired world fame, but at best only the Nobel Prize. Thus, the family's permanent stay in Pribor or his own permanent employment at Brücke's institute, both heartily desired when he had to separate from either, would have obstructed the birth of psychoanalysis. He was the man to bend adversities into blessings.

In order to pursue further the puzzle of the 1878 letter, it is necessary to take note of an exceptional feature in Freud's solution of the oedipal conflict. The age difference between the mother and her firstborn child was almost the same as that between her and the child's father, which made him more like a grandfather than a father, which alone diminished the intensity of conflict. When Freud was ten or twelve the father revealed himself as having been most unheroic in his youth. When he was a young man, he told the boy,

"I went for a walk on Saturday . . . ; I was well dressed, and had a new fur cap on my head. A Christian came up to me and with a single blow knocked off my cap into the mud and shouted: 'Jew! Get off the pavement.' " And what did you do, I asked. "I went into the roadway and picked up my cap," was his quiet reply. This struck me as unheroic conduct on the part of the big strong man who was holding the boy by the hand. (Freud 1900a, 197)

The father's voluntary resignation as an authority-enforcing super-ego[22] which this report implies spared the boy the necessity of acting out his aggression. This abrogation of a paternal ego ideal, which would have led to delinquency in many, did not, in Freud's case, exclude esteem for his father's occasional "admirable unself-ishness" and dream-thoughts in which the father was held up in unqualified admiration as a model (Freud 1900a, 437). The almost-conflict-free dethronement of the father as an ideal in early puberty, when others of that age go through severe crises, has to be noted in order to understand Freud's longing for a reliable father *imago*, his simultaneous distrust of father substitutes, and his marvelous ability to function optimally, no matter what the specific superego conflict might have been at a given time. The disappoint-ment at Stricker's laboratory was only of limited duration; I presume that Freud knew that return to Brücke was always open to him.[23]

Thus, by the time he wrote Knöpfmacher in 1878, he had at last found a satisfactory superego authority figure in Brücke but was, at least temporarily, separated from him. In 1878 four years separated him from the dire moment when he would have to forgo the pleasure of neurohistology for the unwelcome preparation for medical prac-tice. He still was in the middle of all the bliss that according to documentary evidence filled the years at Brücke's institute—"in which I spent the happiest hours of my student life free from all other desires" (Freud 1900a, 206). The days in Brücke's laboratory, where he performed his research, were Freud's halcyon days.[24] There "I found rest and full satisfaction" (1925d, 9)—a strong indica-tion that neurohistology was a potent channel of sublimation and made it possible to evade sexual temptations and conflicts. Indeed, to characterize his experience he used terms which he did not use in any other context. He wrote Martha (26 June 1885) that he carried out his first research as a student with an "unequalled enthusiasm" (*Begeisterung ohnegleichen*). And even as late as 1894, twelve years after Breuer had told him of catharsis and eight years after he had met Charcot, on his thirty-eighth birthday he still called (neuro) anatomy "the only thing that satisfies" (*das einzig Befriedigende*) (6 May 1894).

To get at the genetic root of Freud's fixation to neurohistology, one has to turn to an early experience, one that occurred when he was six years old. Freud mentioned it as an association to a dream. When he was six years old, he was given his first lessons by his mother:

I was expected to believe that we were all made of earth and therefore must return to earth. This did not suit me and I expressed doubts of the doctrine. My mother thereupon rubbed the palms of her hands together . . . and showed me the blackish scales of *epidermis* produced by the friction as a proof that we were made of earth. My astonishment at this ocular demonstration knew no bounds. (1900a, 205)

I can almost see the boy, wide-eyed, looking at his mother, deeply awed by that revelation. In that moment a creative spark struck him, and he became possessed by what would become something like an addiction, the wish to create the same surprise in others by ocular demonstrations of the improbable like the one his mother had produced for him,[25] and he became an inimitable master of ocular demonstrations of the most improbable. He accomplished ocular demonstrations of the secrets buried in the tissues of the central nervous system in Brücke's laboratory, where he did not rub his palms but used the equivalent of epidermal scales to mount beautifully dyed specimens. What was observed in the microscope was even more convincing than the scales of maternal epidermis.

But fate carried him on to even more surprising demonstrations. His interpretations of dreams and his case histories are specimens of that art. Who else but Freud would have been able to demonstrate *ad oculos* that dreams are wish fulfillments and that Schreber's bizarre extravagances are meaningful? And so the passionate little boy's wish was abundantly fulfilled. Still, the ecstasy felt in the first steps he took in making the invisible visible remained unrivaled. Never again would his gaze penetrate the invisible with such clarity as in Brücke's laboratory. And now it will become understandable why he was bound to fail in Stricker's institute as well as in later attempts at experimental work (Jones 1953–1957, 1:54). There it was not a matter of demonstration *ad oculos* but rather a rough and hard process of inferences and guesses essentially different from the classical clarity and beauty of histological slides; whereas physiological observations are almost invariably replaced by better ones, histological observations are permanent.

There is more to be said about the recollection of age six. The mother entered as a gigantic figure knowledgeable in esoteric wisdom. She proved herself to be in the possession of fear-arousing tidings and even carried their proof in the palms of her hands. It was uncanny that such evidence derived from her very body. Did the maternal revelation include her own passing away one day? In the associations to the dream in which the childhood recollection shows up, the imagery of the Three Fates appears, which are figures endowed with immortality; one of them was the mother. There is a triad of opposite provenance drawn from the first novel[26] the youngster had read at age thirteen. He apparently was impressed by its tragic ending, inasmuch as it left a vivid memory. "The hero went mad and kept calling out the names of the three women who had brought greatest happiness and sorrow into his life." Are we to surmise the three Macbeth witches to have been the successors of these three women?

But the mother's crude but irrefutable ocular demonstration of death is, of course, the focal point of the dream. "My astonishment at this ocular demonstration knew no bounds and I acquiesced in the belief which I was later to hear expressed in the words: '*Du bist der Natur einen Tod schuldig*' ("You owe nature a death," which is a transformation of Shakespeare's "Thou owest God a death" (Henry IV, Part I, V/1, l. 127). When Freud replaced "readiness" with *Heiterkeit* in Hamlet, he did it deliberately, but in the latter instance it is not clear whether the alteration was intentional. This same alteration appears in a letter to Fliess of 6 February 1899. I am not convinced that this was a *lapsus calami* because it amounts to the inchoation of the death drive theory. It sounds like a manifesto, a rebellious manifesto, for that matter, a conscious forceful opposition to any debt to God. I believe that Freud did not accept the idea of death as a debt even to nature, although he wrote in a footnote that "astonishment and submission to the inevitable" (1900a, 205, n.2) were attached to the early experience. It cannot be stressed enough that this first conscious encounter with the idea of

death was indelibly rooted in the imagery of an all-powerful, omni-
scient mother. One also must stress that Freud's extraordinary scientific perspicacity is rooted in the creative magic of voyeurism.
The associations to the dream about the Three Fates lift the veil of
forbidden subjects. There are attacks against those whom he re-
vered most, Brücke and Goethe. He dreamed of himself as a thief
and plagiarizer. He averred the philosophy of *carpe diem*—"Do not
think of consequences and grab whatever comes your way." Does it
not sound like Macbeth? Only in this instance a smooth, deceptive
surface covers the heave and surge of the wildest, most forbidden
passions and of disrespect for adults like that of Max and Moritz. It
is remarkable that a dream that occurred decades after the letter to
Knöpfmacher, one in which the consequences of demonstrations *ad
oculos* is a central theme, leads again to the gloomy problem of
death.

Thus, unrestricted exegesis leads to the suspicion that ideas, fears,
and fantasies about death were tied to Freud's exploratory activities from the beginning. Knöpfmacher's recollection of Freud's remark that he felt like the young man in Schiller's poem would
confirm this and at the same time give the reason. To unveil the
secrets of nature is a piece of hubris, a challenge demanding revenge. As a matter of fact, Freud, through his psychoanalytic explorations, uncovered secrets that the Lord, I guess, had preordained
should stay unrevealed at least until shortly before the Last Judgment. But on that afternoon in 1878 when he had restored his
honest name by paying back a debt, he had not yet lent his mind to
sacrilegious pursuits. He still was protected by the authority of his
teacher, who carried responsibility for everything the tyro did. Yet
that teacher had let him down once and Freud had made himself
guilty of falsely taking glory for priority that was not his. More
importantly, the Macbeth reference points to the future, to later
papers. And here the challenging possibility presents itself that
early, when working under Brücke's authority, Freud had a vague
premonition or a vague impulse that his strivings would one day
be directed at deeper wisdom than can be harvested from neurohistology. For that truth he would have to carry responsibility.
Once he was asked by Ludwig Braun, a brother of the B'nai B'rith,

whether he, "the immensely fertile one, is always ready for work." He replied, "When I seat myself to work and take the pen to hand, then I am always curious what will come [on that occasion] and this drives me incessantly to work" (Knöpfmacher 1970, 70). With Freud, the goddess dealt more gently than with his Egyptian forebear, who was stricken by perpetual lack of contentment. She had made Freud her prolocutor. One notes again how neurotic dreads were transformed by him into constructive defenses: the illusion of a "self-writing" book becomes a reality which absolves the writer of guilt and fear of revenge).[27]

The illusion interceded in favor of liberating and stimulating the creative process. The fear of penetrating into forbidden recesses of nature may have been an additional factor in Freud's preference for histology and his long delay in joining Breuer. As a neurohistologist he was under the aegis of an unassailable authority, but when he switched to the vocation of plumbing the mental underground, for a long time he stood alone, deserted even by Breuer, the initiator of the scientific movement Freud would go on to develop. At the risk of repetition I wish to emphasize that Freud's psychoanalytic oeuvre can be called a gigantic demonstration *ad oculos* of the invisible—in psychoanalytic terms, of making what is unconscious conscious.

All the tragic implications I have expatiated here were hidden. To all outward appearances Freud was a happy, promising scientist while he worked as a neurohistologist, earning the friendship and respect of two outstanding men, Josef Breuer and Ernest Fleischl von Marxov (1846–1891). There were many triumphs to follow, among which the greatest was his marriage to Martha Bernays, which for years had seemed improbable. With the use of hypnosis and the development of psychoanalysis he had many occasions of triumphant demonstrations *ad oculos*. But as has been mentioned repeatedly, from 1896 on he was pushed into a corner and had to face an extraordinary opposition comparable only to that which Darwin encountered. But Freud was internally prepared for a hard fight. From Paris he wrote Martha (2 February 1886) that Breuer had discovered in him, behind a covering of shyness, "an immeasurably daring and fearless person." He often had felt "as if I had inherited the whole defiance and all the passion of our ancestors when they defended their temple, as if I could throw down my life with joy for a great moment."[28]

There is evidence that he felt drawn toward opposition and probably enjoyed it. Thus, he wrote, "Even at school I was always the bold oppositionist" (to Martha Bernays, 2 February 1886). And decades later: "[A] certain degree of readiness to accept a situation of solitary opposition" was necessary to create psychoanalysis (Freud 1925e, 222). Yet even a passionate oppositionist will not necessarily cherish a lifelong position of that sort. This would perhaps have been to Karl Marx's taste, but was it to Freud's, who was not only a conquistador but also a tenderly affectionate person who loved and wanted to be loved and receive acknowledgment? These wishes were not fulfilled. As said, his name went on to become a curse word in Western civilization. An infinitesimal small group heralded him as great, but the majority decided that not a single "ocular demonstration" had been accomplished by him.

Whether he was, as an old man, certain that he had attained the ocular demonstration of psychoanalysis or not (after all, he had his doubts about the survival of his psychoanalytic discoveries), he was aware that his early histological discoveries were as true as ever and would remain so as long as man cared to peer through microscopes. He knew that if he had stayed with his first love he might have been awarded the Nobel Prize like Ramon y Cajal (1852–1932), who was made a Nobel laureate in 1906 for his exploration of the finer cerebral structure. This was exactly the area of Freud's main interest at the time when he relinquished neurohistology. He was the true discoverer of the neurone theory, as is evident from a paper he presented in 1882 (1884f.).[29]

Freud's personal ambition, however, was not to obtain the Nobel Prize. When he read that Pater Wilhelm Schmidt,[30] "my chief enemy," had just been given the Medal of Honor for Art and Science, he wrote Arnold Zweig, "When my great Master[31] received this Award[32] I became aware of the wish that I myself might someday attain it" (Jones 1953–1957, 3:208). That wish was still operative, for he wrote: "Fate has its own ways of making me altruistic. . . . Today I contentedly resign myself to having indirectly helped someone else to do so." But at eighty, he knew both that he would never get Brücke's decoration and that had he remained with Brücke, he would have been given it.[33]

A definite sign of tiring of always being in the opposition was reported by Wittels (1924). On the occasion of the Congress in Nuremberg, Freud allegedly addressed a group of analysts who opposed his organizational plan: "I am old and do not always want to be exposed to [nothing] but ill will" *(will mich immer nur angefeindet werden)*. At eighty, he may have felt nostalgia for the fleshpots of Egypt, for if he had stayed with Brücke, a good many other things would have been quite different. He would have spent his working life under peaceful conditions, turning out one paper after another on the secrets of the central nervous system, being praised and admired, essentially in harmony with colleagues and friends. His professional transactions and accomplishments would have hardly aroused bitterness. But what did he get in exchange for having given up the energizing tranquility of the Institute of Physiology? Initially, error after error; finally, discoveries rejected by every decent person, curses as a corruptor of decency, and betrayal by his best friends, who became his adversaries and did not hesitate to malign him. The nation whose language he adored and had enriched by valuable concepts and terms declared his writing anathema and banned and damned them. His works were publicly burned. The day was dawning when his writings would not be available in their original language and no German-speaking person would be permitted to read a word he had written. The movement he had set in motion was filled with dissension, disagreements, mutual reproaches. Were the findings in psychology really that vague or ambiguous? Did they lack entirely that clarity that endowed cerebral histology with a glow of beauty? If one stuck to firmly established rules, one could not lose one's *Heiterkeit* stooped over the microscope; such a loss could happen only when authority enforced a premature publication, and that was a rare exception. But worst of all, what was the true value of his discoveries? Did he not overrate them? Where was the proof of their existence? Much as he might shift his theories around, they did not click. Man remained to him the same enigma he was when he started out to explore him fifty years before. Hardly anything remained of an ocular demonstration.

There is a document that when properly interpreted brings to light a desperate mood Freud felt in old age about his final accomplishments and a vehement longing for the sunniness and joyousness that filled the days at the Institute of Physiology. It seemed that the premonitions evoked by his allusions to Macbeth and Busch in 1878 had been on the mark. I refer to an episode that strikes the reader as paradoxical and bizarre at first hearing.

R. Brun (1885–1969), the first to pay serious attention to Freud's biological and neurological research, wrote a paper about Freud's prepsychoanalytic work (Brun 1936). He described the great accomplishments of the young scientist and drew commendable inferences which can by no means be called exaggerated; if anything, I believe that today Freud's preanalytic writings would meet with even greater approval.[34] When he answered Brun (18 March 1936), Freud thanked him for the effort he had made "on behalf of my 'organic' works." However, he continued, "I am *startled* [my emphasis] by the tribute [*Würdigung*] which you seem to accord them, for I know, most of them are of little worth, a few, however, are of no worth at all" (*die meisten von ihnen taugen wenig, einige aber gar nichts*). He stated that he would enumerate those of no worth, "of course with the request not to make the condemning judgment public with an all too loud voice" (*mit der Bitte, das verdammende Urteil nicht allzu laut bekannt zu machen*). (Here there is an intimation of Gath and Askelon.) And then he proceeded to tear his early publications to pieces—including, in fact, one he had mentioned pridefully to Knöpfmacher fifty-eight years earlier. He went so far as to call "moronic" *(läppisch)* the paper on the lobed organs of the eel (which later was highly praised, as will be seen), making a pun on the word *Lappenorgane (lobed organs)*. He asked to be pardoned: "I was 20 years old and my teacher, the zoologist Claus, was negligent enough not to check that work, which was my first." He wondered how in view of his later "severity" *(Strenge)* he could have been so "frivolous" *(leichtfertig)*, and he continued to demolish one paper after another, ending with the hardly believable statement, "I have the feeling that in addition I should apologize to you" *(ich habe die Empfindung ich müsste Sie auch noch um Entschuldigung bitten)*.

Here we reencounter in the old man something comparable to

the feeling of apprehension which Macbeth had felt when contemplating future kings. That Freud had to struggle with such feelings is all the more tragic because he did not know to the end of his life that his first paper on the mysterious organ of the eel was an outstanding accomplishment—as the praise of a man whose disposition toward Freud was not friendly bears witness (Gicklhorn 1955).[35] No doubt, no one could have dealt with the young Freud in a rougher way than the eighty-year-old himself. He conducted a devastating court proceeding against his youthful years. One asks what the conscious and unconscious motives could have been that made Freud feel so devastatingly destructive toward his youthful work when as a matter of fact it was deserving of high praise. It really sounds like the peak of cynicism hatched out in the brain of a malicious biographer who cannot miss an opportunity to belittle Freud when he himself stated that the new method he discovered to study the course of fibers (Freud 1884b, 1884c) "was in fact *good,* but proved itself as *completely unreliable [völlig unzuverlässig],* so that I myself had to give it up" (my emphasis), as if he were incapable of tolerating a favorable comment. When his youthful creations offend the taste of the accomplished mature genius, as happened to Goethe after he had outgrown the wild years of *Sturm und Drang* and reached the peak of the classic style, critical comments about youthful excesses would be understandable. But such considerations do not apply to the old Freud. His youthful style had been impeccable, no less so than that of later years, and from the beginning he was loyal to the principles for whose realization he would continue to exert himself for the rest of his life: enlarging knowledge of empirical fact and endeavoring to make theoretical inferences on the highest level of abstraction.

Upon reading Brun's words of high praise for his youthful exploits, Freud's regret over their loss might have been not merely activated but vigorously intensified.[36] In other words, he felt a wave of nostalgia, an intense longing to reexperience the joy of those early days, and an angry feeling that he had been cheated out of the possibility of making neurohistology his permanent calling. The defense in the form of vehement self-denigration might then have been provoked, as if he wanted to be certain beyond any doubt: "It was no good what I did in those foolish years and it would have led only to rubbish. The course my life took was actually the best possible and I have reason only to be grateful."

Brun's commendation must have hurt deeply. Here was a testimony to the superiority of his early work. In that moment Freud turned against his early successes in a rage. Like Macbeth he felt that the witches had cheated him by luring him away from the right path and making him aspire to forbidden fruit. The content of Freud's letter to Brun is plainly absurd. Freud himself advised that one treat such instances of the absurd in the same way as equivalent dream-elements are treated (letter to James S. H. Bransom [1934]; see Jones 1953–1957, 3:458); he pointed out that the absurd represents "embittered criticism and contemptuous contradiction" (Freud 1905c, 175). The feeling that he was cheated out of happiness and that he should have stayed at the Institute is made inoperative by the absurd thought that everything he had produced there was ridiculous nonsense. One sometimes gets angry at happiness lost through one's own actions.[37] The other consideration, that the rage at his neurohistological work was a displacement of a deep disappointment in psychoanalysis, would be relevant for a meaningful biography of Freud.

For many years, indeed, the rebellion against Brücke and the turn toward the recondite, despite the multifarious conflicts and snares that awaited him in that territory, reaped rich harvests. The illusion of the self-writing book brought high dividends; but then followed book burning, withholding of honors he aspired to as a young man, doubt in the permanence of his findings, the extreme forms analysis took with followers present and past. For each such occurrence when taken by itself, an excuse could be found: to be on the list of "burned" authors was in itself an honor; it was bearable not to be honored in a state that was dominated by political reaction and church.

But Freud was always tormented by misgivings about the future of psychoanalysis. There was no reason to call in question the future of biology. A harassing doubt, however, hovered over the fate of psychoanalysis. His demonstrations *ad oculos* had not worked. He wrestled with that problem in the thirty-fourth of his *Lectures* (1933a). It seemed to refute basic conclusions that men like Adler and Jung, who had practiced psychoanalysis, acknowledged its truth content, and had added substantially to it, could nevertheless reach the point of writing as if they never had heard of psychoanalysis. It became indisputable that no unified field would be left by his efforts and that what was envisioned as psychoanalysis would decay into schools separated irreconcilably. All this together made— at least for a moment but probably with increasing weight, at age eighty—the recollection of neurohistology, which had been free of all these complications, extremely attractive. In order to evade the beauty of the seductive memory of the Garden of Eden, it had to be cursed.

May I repeat: Brun's essay aroused the longing for Egypt's fleshpots. After decades of tumultuous psychological research, scruples, revisions, isolation, fights, and abuse, those early years of neurology appeared in an exalted, radiant light, almost surrounded by a halo. They were irretrievable, and when Freud was assured that his neurological achievements had been eminent, he had to fight off a depression filled with remorse. Rage serves such a purpose.

If the four quotations I elaborated on, one from the Bible about the silence to be kept in the streets, and three from Shakespeare— Macbeth facing the collapse of his hopes, Macbeth's death, and Hamlet approaching his death in serenity—are viewed together, one is struck by the facts that two refer to a time when the hero approaches death and two to a time when he is exposed to an extreme calamity.[38] This seems to suggest that Freud had an unconscious, covert, but perhaps constantly activated feeling of being close to death or a calamity of a comparable kind. The inferences I drew from quotations Freud used may be called extreme, perhaps even unwarranted, particularly when I suggest that they indicate the existence of a chronically operative attitude, a chronic threat, a kind of thorn in the flesh, which caused something like an irritation which had to be met, denied, or made inoperative, as the case may be, by a stream of production of highest values.

Still, if my suggestion that there was operative in Freud a chronic potential pain which was a derivative of covert anticipation of a calamity should contain a grain of truth, it may explain two of his peculiarities. As has been repeatedly pointed out, particularly by those seeking to ridicule Freud, he was preoccupied with the fanciful yearning to figure out the year of his death. If there remained in him an infantile anxiety about a calamity such as having to leave abruptly, as happened at age three, which would be comparable to death, this would explain the recurrent attempt at figuring out the year of that future calamity. Once that date had been determined, the vague fears would temporarily be structured; an otherwise unbroken line of time would be divided by focal points. With the creation of such an illusion of mastery, chronic anxiety would be concentrated upon a few nodal points, rather than fill extended periods of time; in the intervals, relative security would be granted.

My suggestion may also help to elucidate a peculiar symptom, if one may call it that. Freud from time to time spoke of the favorable effect physical malaise had on his productivity. Physical well-being over longer periods of time reduced the likelihood of a creative outflow. A very radical description of that peculiarity is found in a letter to Fliess: "At present I am free of pain, which is exceptional; when I am well, I am terribly lazy" (7 July 1898). It was not a matter of an actual disease, to which he would not have responded favorably, but of ill-defined discomfort of a type that did not mark the inception of a physical illness. I thought of it as a masochistic response, but Freud, despite occasional self-destructive steps, was not a masochist. The hypothesis of an inner irritation that had to be allayed by creativity would make the necessity of discomfort better understandable. Physical well-being would mean that the irritation had been quieted by physiological processes or whatnot. In Breuer's terms, energy—in this instance destructive rather than libidinal—would have become bound and lost its irritating effect. Functional malaise, on the other hand, would, again in Breuer's terms, indicate that the bound energy had become free-floating and was accumulating. The malaise would signal that sufficient energy had been activated to initiate and accelerate the creative process. Libido advances the self toward the world and heightens the pleasure and joy derived from it; a destructive impulse, small as ever it may be, is necessary to effect a step back and form the wish to make the world better than it is by one's own doing. Freud put it into general terms when he wrote to Marie Bonaparte, "All activities that rearrange or effect changes are to a certain extent destructive and thus redirect a portion of the instinct [drive] from its original destructive goal" (Jones 1953–1957, 3:464). A covert fear of dying would keep destructive impulses alive and thus be a secret font of creation. The creation of values actually postpones death. The more Aristotle could create, the more of him would survive, and the longer would be the period of time during which he would be read and admired. In many people's—perhaps everyone's—imagination, death occurs ultimately only when one is no longer remembered by anyone. Freud conceded that to a writer "immortality evidently means being loved by many unknown people" (p. 465). Macbeth in the kingly ghosts' encounter was despairing about facing "real" death because of his lack of progeny. Was the young Freud worried that his papers would not secure the love of many succeeding generations? Certainly Max and Moritz were pranksters whose death everyone welcomed and no one mourned.

Death may appear in many forms. What might have been the core of Freud's unconscious image of that anticipated calamity? After Pfister visited in May 1909, Freud thanked him (letter, 10 May 1909) for the advice not to work too much. When a patient left him, he did not replace him, "and since then I felt well and happy and admit that you were right. . . . My own father complex, as Jung would call it, that is, the need to correct my father would never have permitted it" (Freud to Pfister, in Freud 1963, 24). Evidently the father's failure as a provider had aroused anxiety that persisted in the adult. On other occasions this was expressed with equal clarity:

My railroad phobia . . . was a fantasy of impoverishment or better a hunger-phobia dependent on my infantile gluttony. (Freud to Fliess, 21 December 1899 in Freud 1985)

From my youth I know that the wild horses in the Pampas that once have been captured with the lasso, have throughout their lives something nervous. So I have become acquainted with helpless poverty and fear it all the time. You will see my style will improve and my ideas [Einfälle] [become] more correct when this city provides me with the means of living well. (21 September 1899)

According to these occasional remarks, the feared calamity was death by famine, a sudden catastrophe that would reduce his capacity for earning and make him destitute.[39] This unconscious imagery, an uneasy source of irritation, was, I believe, a force that propelled him toward mental creative action. When it was not operative and the body provided only feelings of well-being, a standstill was brought about. But the activation of displeasure—which in simplified fashion may be called creative hunger—provided the energy required by channels of creation in order to become productive.[40] How intensely in Freud's outlook sufferings and creativity were associated becomes impressively clear in the letter in which he congratulated his friend Fliess on his fortieth birthday (23 October 1898). He wished among other things that he should stay free of any trace of suffering and sickness beyond what "man urgently needs for bracing his energies."[41]

At last, when the messenger of death intruded into Freud's existence and death became a concrete reality, true serenity was achieved. Though reduced in number by grave illness and old age, his creative outpourings never reached a standstill. Death was finally enforced by Freud's own decision when the body denied any pleasure and became nothing but a bucket of pain. Perhaps he would have been ready to tolerate even such tribulations if his dog had not been repelled by the graveolency of cancer that had perforated the body's surface. But that final decision occurred in the midst of composing his *Outline of Psychoanalysis* (1940a), that magnificent survey of his discoveries' final shape that reads like a king's chart of his realm. Yet was it ever intended to be a kind of farewell address, or did it become one accidentally in the unbearable surge of agony? During the years of the First World War, Freud took stock in the extended form of his lectures before he went about the basic restructuring of his theories from 1920 on. Was the *Outline* a comparable stock-taking, as if he needed a firm foothold, like on a rock on which to stand, in order to produce a radical reform of psychoanalysis? Freud was a restless thinker. He knew that "doubt cannot be detached from science," as he wrote Stefan Zweig in 1937 (Freud 1960; letter of 17 October)—that is, he was only too aware of the temporality of his findings and theories, but I venture to speculate that he wanted to shoot the arrow as far as possible. Fifteen years had gone by since *The Ego and the Id,* and so a call for a new overhaul would have been ripe.

I have the impression that Freud was in the process of what I should tentatively call remodeling or extending psychoanalytic ego pathology.

The last section of the unfinished *Outline* is devoted to the splitting of the ego. Splitting was called a state in which two parts are marked off. They are equivalent but of opposite meaning, one an affirmation of the existence of something, and the other an affirmation of its nonexistence. This disjunction, however, does not lead to conflict or controversy and is not perceived as a contradiction. It evidently is different from repression. The kind of splitting Freud had in mind is probably indispensable for survival in a culture that is far too complex and contradictory for integration. But although splitting might make survival possible, at the same time it would be a basic obstacle to function as an equilibrated, reliable organization. I would compare the basic ego splitting to Newton's basic law of action and reaction. One of them is often difficult to observe but always present.

If there should be truth in my speculation that Freud intended to lay the foundation of a new ego pathology, a delay in his demise would have brought an incalculable harvest. What the modifications and new shoots actually would have been remains concealed, but they would have postponed for long the rut that unavoidably is formed when a science that does not grow on technology is left without genius.

As we have seen, the two quotations from *Macbeth* and the one from *Hamlet* in between form a formidable biographical triangle in a period of Freud's life that resonates and gives token of his dazzling creativity. I have extended that triangle's area by adding the mother's ocular demonstration as the spark that set the child's dormant genius aflame, his father's conflict-free dethronement, which gave freedom of choice of ego ideal, and finally the old man's curse at age eighty.

It is striking that after comprehensive recourse to unrestricted exegesis, in the end, the way leads to a document, the letter to Brun. It would be particularly gratifying if the wide-ranging explorations and the document concur, or at least converge. It must be stressed that in this undertaking hardly at any point was recourse taken to common sense, and indeed, each interpretation may have offended common-sense thinking.

Two further comments are necessary regarding unrestricted exegesis and common-sense, or traditional, psychology.

1. The reader may feel unconvinced when I draw attention here and there to the gap between common-sense psychology and psychoanalysis. Indeed, the demonstration of its full extent would fill a thick, dry tome. Here, substantiation by an anecdote, ably recounted by Elms (1990), is preferable. In his "callow youth" Gordon Allport (?–1967), then twenty-two and already strongly interested in psychological science, whose graduate study he would soon direct at Harvard, wrote Freud, then sixty-four, "a note announcing that I was in Vienna and no doubt he would be glad to see me." Freud responded with an invitation to visit. In Freud's office, Allport, "not prepared for [Freud's] silence . . . fished around in my mind and . . . told him about an episode on the tramcar coming out." It concerned "a little boy about four years old" who "obviously was developing a real dirt phobia." Allport "thought it might interest Freud how early a phobia of dirt can get set. He listened, and fixed his therapeutic eye upon me, and said. 'Was that little boy you?' Honestly, it wasn't, but I felt guilty."

The psychological sequelae of this episode were evidently profound, perhaps even exerting a major influence on the Harvard professor's 1937 textbook on personality. Forty-four years after his meeting with Freud, in an interview, Allport said, "[A]ctually [Freud] mistook my motives. If he had said, 'Well, here is a brassy young American youth, a tourist who is imposing on my good nature and time,' he would have been somewhere near correct, I think. But to ascribe my motivation to the unconscious in this case was definitely wrong." The passage suggests that Allport's meeting with Freud had a seminal role in the budding of the common-sense psychologist. There can be hardly any doubt that Allport was wrong in denying that Freud regarded him as a "brassy young American." What else could Freud have thought? Freud was too civilized to put such a sentiment into words. Moreover, there would have been no contradiction between Freud's perceiving his visitor to be "a brassy young American" and asking the clinician's question: "Was that little boy you?" Allport commented upon his meeting with Freud on other occasions, repeating his denial of Freud's insight. Elms, however, in his biographical essay on Allport, had no difficulty in proving that Allport was indeed "that little boy." At the same time, he demonstrated how the twenty-two-year-old's denial ("Honestly, it wasn't") evolved into the "theory of functional autonomy," the thesis that "motivation was often functionally autonomous of its historical origins in life."

One could not imagine a more dramatic illustration of the gap between psychoanalysis and traditional thinking. At the same time one is moved to remark that the autonomy of the theory of functional autonomy is jeopardized by Elms's findings—and with it, the foundation of Allport's version of common-sense psychology.

2. My use of unrestricted exegesis may have given the reader the impression that the totality of the unconscious, in my view, is, so to speak, "buried" in each single cultural element, and that the "good" interpreter has the faculty (and obligation) to tease out, item by item, hidden meanings, making optimal use of his own unconscious as well as of every cultural deposit within his purview. These propositions may be ridiculed if they are construed as amounting to the allegation that "everything is contained in, or linked to everything else." There might indeed be justice to a critical remark of that sort. This criticism would not be justified, had I not neglected a companion proposition that has to do with the "criterion of fitness." This standard limits possible interpretations to those that are suitable in specific contexts. The connection between the element to be interpreted and the interpreter's response consists of a chain of events that are mostly unconscious and have not yet been sufficiently explored. Once the intricacies of that pathway have been clarified, the likelihood of derailments will be significantly curtailed because the interpreter will possess a tool that can be used to avoid them. The reader should bear in mind, finally, that documents are eyewitnesses one has to respect although even they may mislead at times. A conscientious interpreter will return over and over again to the eyewitnesses of the act to be interpreted, and check their reliability. But the importance of the proper use (in the psychoanalytic sense) of documents cannot be overrated.

Even so hazardous a proposition as the one that Freud felt nostal-

gic for the years in the Institute of Physiology and therefore regretted involvement in psychoanalysis gains greatly in probability
when his letter to Abraham of 21 September 1924 is considered: "It
is making severe demands on the unity of the personality to try and
make me identify myself with the author of the paper on the spinal
ganglia of the petromyzon. Nevertheless I must be he, and I think I
was happier about that discovery than about others since." This
was written twelve years before he put his neurological papers
under a ban.

I have been roving around in this discourse and of course do not
know which parts if any may be accepted and confirmed by others,
but even if my efforts may be proved to have been in vain, I anticipate that at least one inference can be drawn reliably regarding
Freud's biography: that his two childhood experiences, the three
identifications, and the curse form a kind of keystone. Or one may
look at them as an arc that has to serve as the prolegomena of a
Freud biography that aspires to meaningfulness. That arc, when
understood, would provide at least faint traces of knowledge about
the processes in that unknown world out of which great ones form
their imperishable ideas.

A strange, thought-provoking autobiographical passage by Goethe,
with whom Freud had so much in common, comes to mind:

> But that I strove to work through what, beyond my strength, I had laid
> my hands on and strove to deserve that which I had obtained beyond my
> deserts, by this only did I differ from the truly insane.[42] First I was for
> people troublesome through my error, then through my steadfastness.
> I might position myself as I wanted, I was alone.[43]

Notes

1. Krüll (1979) is an exception, but an autobiographical passage by
   Freud which she overlooked invalidates her main conclusion.
2. Fritz Heider may be cited as an authority who upholds the superiority
   of a "common-sense" psychology. He was praised warmly by Snelbecker (1988), who declared that "Heider's contributions have been

comprehensive and unique, particularly concerning relations between 'scientific' psychology and 'common sense' psychology." Heider is quoted as believing that "scientific psychology has a good deal to learn from common-sense psychology. . . . [F]ruitful concepts and hunches lie dormant and unformulated in what we know intuitively."

3. Freud used this quotation in an earlier letter, as discussed below.
4. Eschenröder (1984, 46) maintains that this remark means: "Although I now know better, I shall conceal from my colleagues that the discovery of the cause of hysteria was founded on a grave error." Some might understand Eschenröder's statement as implying fraudulent intention on Freud's part, but such a reading can safely be dismissed. Freud knew well that his 1896 paper (1896c) had not induced a single soul to practice the therapy he had suggested in it. Furthermore, a patient would not be harmed by an exploration as to the possibility of early sexual abuse.
5. Freud 1960a, ed. 2, p. 15. The occasion of 1880 is noteworthy. After Freud had passed his examination in pharmacology, he told his friend Carl Koller (1857–1944) that just before that ordeal, he had given up hope of not failing; but under the anticipation of his friends' singing David's mournful song after his failure, "I decided to descend into the depth of pharmacology for 12 more hours." In this instance he used the quotation to spur himself to constructive action and, thereby, to avoid defeat.
6. From this occasion as well as from the above-cited possibility of a flunked examination, one learns that the Askelon episode came to Freud's mind when he was considering something highly distressing, something that either had just happened or might take place in the near future.
7. I shall not praise psychoanalysts' reliability in dealing with documents because all too often they have jumped to the conclusions they preferred, neglecting documents that would disprove their interpretations or greatly reduce their probability. The extent to which Freud neglected documents is an interesting subject for study. In general, Freud was attracted by the documentary aspect of research in the humanities, but he was reproached for uncritical use of secondary literature in composing *Totem and Taboo*, the *Leonardo* study, and the *Moses* book. His failure to gather and avail himself of data on Schreber's father (cf. Freud 1911c) was also held against him as a serious omission, but that criticism is not well grounded.
8. His feeling of guilt about the infant brother's death contributed, if anything, to Freud's devotion to his ten-year younger brother, whom he loved affectionately. This is not the only instance of Freud's converting neurotic conflict into constructive action.
9. Freud was quite ready to adapt quotations to inner needs; cf. p. 47.

10. How deeply Hamlet's "special providence" was embedded in Freud's own unconscious may be conjectured from a passage that to my ear contains a confessional innuendo—his reference to the "dark power of Destiny which only the fewest of us are able to look upon as impersonal" (1924c, 168).

11. Knöpfmacher was Freud's B'nai B'rith brother as well as a close friend. In a letter that has been lost, Freud said of him that "he has destroyed his childhood belief" (*er ihm den Kinderglauben genommen habe;* Knöpfmacher 1970, 58). On another occasion Freud called Knöpfmacher "his dear school friend" (p. 60). I mention these details because they evoke the picture of intimacy, which would explain why Freud revealed to him details of a particularly personal and private nature. For Knöpfmacher and his relationship to Freud, see the article by Knöpfmacher's son, Hugo Knöpfmacher (1970).

12. In documents originating in an early developmental phase of maturation, a creative person sometimes divulges basic conflicts and problems that later become concealed.

13. Literally, "spirit" *(Geist).*

14. My translation. Freud wrote *Jüngster Tag,* that is, "youngest day," which meant "doomsday" or Last Judgment.

15. On 1 September 1911, Freud wrote to Jung, "Perhaps all in all it is better 'to die in harness' " (McGuire 1974, 271; the words within single quotation marks were in English).

16. The German *necken* also carries an affectionate connotation; *was sich liebt, dass neckt sich,* as a German saying has it.

17. Die, anstatt durch weise Lehren/ Sich zum Guten zu bekehren,/ Oftmals noch darüber lachten/ Und sich heimlich lustig machten.—/ —Ja, zur Übeltätigkeit,/ Ja, dazu ist man bereit!—/—Menschen necken, Tiere quälen,/ Äpfel, Birnen, Zwetschken stehlen— / Das ist freilich angenehmer/ Und dazu auch viel bequemer,/ Als in Kirche oder Schule/ Festzusitzen auf dem Stuhle.—/ —Aber wehe, wehe, wehe / Wenn ich auf das Ende sehe!!—/ Ach, das war ein schlimmes Ding,/ Wie es Max und Moritz ging.

18. However, at age nineteen Freud wrote his friend Silberstein that he had changed his ideal from that of a scholar to that of a practicing physician who longs for "a Great Hospital and plenty of money in order to retrench some of the maladies that affect our body" (Freud 1989, 144).

19. To my feeling the original German *anklagen* is a nuance stronger than "to accuse."

20. I owe thanks to Professor Gerhard Fichtner for the information that no biographical data about Kutschin are available.

21. Freud received his medical diploma in 1881 after a delay of approximately two years.

22. One may speak of the transformation of Freud's perception of his father brought about by the story of the unheroic act as a reverse (negative) epiphany.

23. It would be important to know the reasons for Freud's half-year stay with Stricker, and what Freud's relationship with the Institute of Physiology was during that period.

24. Freud was inclined to focus on the bliss of nodal situations and disregard discordant elements. Thus he referred to the first three years of his life as cloudless, being the eldest son of a youthful mother and enjoying nature in the countryside of his birthplace (1931e, 259). But did he not acquire during that time a lifelong feeling of guilt as a result of his death wishes against a younger brother who died in infancy? At Brücke's institute, too, there were clouds, in the form of tensions among talented, ambitious researchers impatiently waiting for advancement (Freud 1900a, 484f.). In the 1878 letter one learns of Freud's anxiety that he might be accused of plagiarism and the conflict-arousing stay in Stricker's laboratory.

25. Some authors connect Freud's creativity with his father's dire prediction that his son, who was six or seven years old at the time, "will come to nothing," a frightful blow to the youngster's ambition (Freud 1900a, 216). In accordance with their makeup, those authors equate ambition and creativity, which is a grave error. In the lives of geniuses that happen to be richly documented, one might find similar experiences that stun the child as came to pass in that felicitous moment of the mother's ocular demonstration. The equivalent occurrence in Goethe's life was his mother's continuing on the following evening, to the boy's unending surprise and delight, the stories she had started to tell the day before, following exactly the plot the little boy had anticipated. This seemingly telepathic coincidence has a very sober explanation. The boy's grandmother, to whom he told his fancies, served as a conduit. I can hardly imagine more effective stimulation of a child for great literary accomplishments (given its possession of the requisite talents).

26. Freud insisted that he never knew its name or author. The identification of the novel would have some biographical import, but my attempt to establish it was unsuccessful.

27. How seriously Freud probably meant that remark may be suspected from a remote echo of that image in his Moses book. "Unluckily," he wrote, "an author's creative power does not always obey his will: the work proceeds as it can, and often presents itself to the author as something independent or even alien" (1939a, 104). About twenty years earlier he had already remarked that even so simple a matter as the arrangement of a piece of writing does not come off as the author intended (1916–1917, 379).

28. Here a countenance different from that in the letter of 1878—even

though one made visible by the influence of cocaine—comes to the fore. Both the identification with Macbeth and that with the Maccabees harbored its own peculiar danger. His constitution had provided Freud with an unusually high potential of sublimation. He was capable of replacing the brutal and dirty affairs of reality with peaceful mental provinces. If there had not been strong dams against acting out passions, he might have easily been overwhelmed by them and his life might have ended in a disaster comparable to that of Macbeth or the two delinquent boys.

29. Freud has not received recognition for his contribution to the neurone theory. Waldeyer-Hartz (1836–1921), who in 1891 employed the term "neurone" for the first time, is usually credited with its discovery. See Jones's account (1953–1957, 1:50).

30. Schmidt (1868–1954), professor of ethnology at the University of Vienna and founder of the Viennese school of ethnology, was closely connected with the Vatican. Schmidt was an ardent opponent of psychoanalysis. It was through his influence that the publication of psychoanalytic literature in Italy was prohibited.

31. In the English version (Jones 1953–57, 3:208) it says "my Master Ernest Brücke," which deprives the passage of the awe and admiration the old man still felt.

32. I am indebted to Dr. Ulrich Weinzierl for the information that Brücke received the Imperial-Royal Austrian-Hungarian badge of honor for Art and Science on 10 April 1888.

33. As matters turned out, his daughter Anna was eventually decorated with it.

34. Recently Professor Fichtner maintained that Freud's preanalytic papers prove that if Freud had not originated psychoanalysis, he nevertheless would have made great discoveries. Fichtner also remarked that if one wants to understand and interpret Freud's achievements as a psychologist, one has to examine his biological work (Fichtner 1987).

35. In a personal communication Gicklhorn praised Freud's paper even more than in print. Freud's perception and description were surprisingly accurate for a beginner, more so than Syrski's. Szymon Syrski (1824–1882) was professor of zoology at Lwow (the old Lemberg in Austria-Hungary). An experienced biologist, Syrski was the first to describe the lobed organ of the eel. Freud's endurance of effort in dissecting four hundred eels cannot be overrated, according to Gicklhorn. The tools at the disposal of a histologist were primitive and the dissections required labor and patience hardly imaginable at present. But most surprising, according to Gicklhorn, was Freud's anticipating the modern view of the eel's lobed organ, that is, that it possesses the potential of developing into the sexual structure of either sex and is in that sense bisexual.

36. A secret, subterranean current of longing for the years of biology may lie at the bottom of one of Freud's remarks in which he predicted a future in which all of his psychological findings would find a description in terms of brain physiology.
37. A comparable response is found in an epithalamium which Freud composed in late adolescence. When Gisela, whom he loved as a youngster, married, he portrayed her as grotesque in a poem purportedly praising her (Freud 1989).
38. In this connection Freud's rejection of the identification with the dying Faust (2 November 1895) may be cited.
39. Bernfeld once told an amusing story. Anna Freud allegedly had compared her home with that of piano teachers who, at the beginning of each season, worry whether they will be able to fill all their hours. Similarly, when Freud and his daughter emigrated, so it was said, they were not certain that they would find sufficient work abroad.
40. Freud's fear of famine should have caused him to evolve a miser's disposition. Yet just the opposite was observed. One of the few great pleasures he indulged in consisted in giving gifts. His generosity and inventiveness in that respect were considerable. Again, a malum was transformed in his life into a bonum.
41. In his next letter (30 October 1898) Freud called that wish nonsensical. It was particularly embarrassing since he had overlooked Fliess's announcement of an impending surgical procedure.
42. A freer translation might run as follows: "Only two traits distinguished me from the truly insane: I tried to work through everything I had taken on, even though it was beyond my strength, and I endeavored to deserve what I had received that went beyond my deserts."
43. "Aber dass ich das über meine Kräfte Ergriffene durchzuarbeiten, das über mein Verdienst Erhaltene zu verdienen suchte, dadurch unterschied ich mich bloss von einem wahrhaft Wahnsinnigen.

    Erst war ich den Menschen unbequem durch meinen Irrtum, dann durch meinen Ernst. Ich mochte mich stellen, wie ich wollte, so war ich allein."

References

Brun, R. 1936. Sigmund Freuds Leistungen auf dem Gebiete der organischen Neurologie. *Schweiz. Archiv f. Neurologie und Psychiatrie* 37:200–207.

Elms, A. 1990. Allport's *Personality* and Allport's personality. In K. Craik, R. Hogan, and R. Wolfe, eds.: *Perspectives in Personality*, vol. 4. Greenwich, Conn.: JAI Press.

Eschenröder, C. T. 1984. *Hier irrte Freud*. Munich, Vienna, and Baltimore: Urban und Schwarzenberg.

Fichtner, G. 1987. Unbekannte Arbeiten von Freud—Schätze im Keller. *Medizinhist. J.* 22, issue 2.

Freud, S. 1877a. Über den Ursprung der hinteren Nervenwurzeln in Rückenmarke von Ammocoetes (Petromyzon Planeri). *S.B. Akad. Wiss. Wien (Math.-Naturwiss. Kl.)*, III. Abt., 75:15–27.

_____. 1877b. Beobachtungen über Gestaltung and feineren Bau der als Hoden beschriebenen Lappenorgane des Aals. *S.B. Akad. Wiss. Wien (Math.-Naturwiss. Kl.)*, I. Abt., 75(4):419–431.

_____. 1878a. Über Spinalganglien und Rückenmarke des Petromyzon. *S.B. Akad. Wiss. Wien (Math.-Naturwiss. Kl.)*, III. Abt., 78(2):81–167.

_____. 1882a. *Über den Bau der Nervenfasern und Nervenzellen beim Flusskrebs. S.B. Akad. Wiss. Wien (Math.-Naturwiss. Kl.)*, III Abt., 85:9.

_____. 1884b. Eine neue Methode zum Studium des Fasever laufer im Centralnervensystem. *Zentralbl. med. Wiss.* 22:16–17.

_____. 1884c. A new histological method for the study of nerve-tracts in the brain and spinal cord [in English]. *Brain* 7:86.

_____. 1884f. Die Struktur der Elemente des Nervensystems. *Jb. Psychiat., Neurol.* 5(3):221.

_____. 1896a. Heredity and the aetiology of the neuroses. *S.E.* 3:143–156.

_____. 1896b. Further remarks on the neuro-psychoses of defence. *S.E.* 3:162–185.

_____. 1896c. The aetiology of hysteria. *S.E.* 3:191–221.

_____. 1897b. Abstracts of the scientific writings of Dr. Sigm. Freud 1877–1897. *S.E.* 3:225–257.

_____. 1900a. The interpretation of dreams. *S.E.* 4:1–338, 5:339–714.

_____. 1905e. Fragment of an analysis of a case of hysteria. *S.E.* 7:1–122.

_____. 1911c. Psycho-analytic notes on an autobiographical account of a case of paranoia (dementia paranoides). *S.E.* 12:1–82.

_____. 1915e. The unconscious. *S.E.* 14:161–204.

_____. 1916d. Some character-types met with in psycho-analytic work. *S.E.* 14:311–333.

_____. 1916–1917. Introductory lectures on psycho-analysis. *S.E.* 15, 16.

_____. 1918b. From the history of an infantile neurosis. *S.E.* 17:7–122.

_____. 1924c. The economic problem of masochism. *S.E.* 19:157–170.

_____. 1925d. An autobiographical study. *S.E.* 20:7–74.

_____. 1925e. The resistances to psycho-analysis. *S.E.* 19:213–222.

_____. 1931e. Letter to the Burgomaster of Pribor. *S.E.* 21:259.

_____. 1933a. New introductory lectures on psycho-analysis. *S.E.* 22:5–182.

_____. 1936a. A disturbance of memory on the Acropolis. *S.E.* 22:237–248.

_____. 1939a. Moses and monotheism: Three essays. *S.E.* 23:1–137.

_____. 1940a. An outline of psychoanalysis. *S.E.* 23:141–207.

———. 1960a. *Briefe 1873–1939*. Ed. E. L. Freud. Frankfurt am Main: Fischer, 1969.

———. 1963: *Psychoanalysis and Faith: The Letters of Sigmund Freud and Oskar Pfister*. Ed. H. Meng and E.L. Freud. New York: Basic Books.

———. 1985. *Briefe an Wilhelm Fliess, 1887–1904. Vollständige Ausgabe*. Frankfurt: S. Fischer Verlag.

———. 1989. *Briefe an Eduard Silberstein*. Frankfurt: S. Fischer Verlag.

Gicklhorn, J. 1955. Wissenschafts geschichtlehre Notizen zu den Studien von S. Syrski (1874) und S. Freud (1877) über männliche Flussbaale. *S.B. Österr. Akad. Wiss. (Math.-Naturwiss. Kl.)*, Abt. I, 164(1 and 2).

Harrison, E. R. 1984. The dark night-sky riddle: A "paradox" that resisted solution. *Science* 226:941–945.

Jones, E. 1953–1957. *The Life and Work of Sigmund Freud*, vols. 1–3. New York: Basic Books.

Knöpfmacher, H. 1970. Zwei Beitrage zur Biographie Freuds. *Jahrbuch der Psychoanalyse* 11:51–72, 1979.

Krüll, M. 1979. *Freud und sein Vater*. Munich: Beck.

Masson, J. M. 1984. *The Assault on Truth: Freud's Suppression of the Seduction Theory*. New York: Farrar, Straus and Giroux.

McGuire, W., ed. 1974. *The Freud/Jung Letters: The Correspondence between Sigmund Freud and C. G. Jung*. Bollingen Series 94. Princeton, N.J.: Princeton University Press.

Shengold, L. 1971. Freud and Joseph. In *The Unconscious Today*, ed. M. Kanzer. New York: International Universities Press.

Snelbecker, G. E. 1988. Letter to the editor: Heider's comprehensive contributions. *Contemp. Psychol.* 33:925.

Stricker, S. 1879a. Über die Leistungen der azinösen Drüsen. *Wiener medizinische Presse* 20:1404–1406.

———. 1879b. Die Leistungen der azinösen Drüsen. *Wiener medizinische Wochenschrift* 29:1133–1134.

Wittels, F. (1924). *Sigmund Freud*. Vienna: E. P. Tal Verlag.

8

Thoughts Stimulated by Preparing Comments on Dr. Eissler's Presentation

George H. Pollock

I am grateful to Emanuel Garcia and the Freud Literary Heritage Foundation for their invitation to discuss Kurt Eissler's rich presentation. Dr. Eissler's courage, devotion, honesty, and meticulous scholarship are a model and an ideal for psychoanalytic researchers. In addition, this new foundation, in which Dr. Eissler and Dr. Garcia have played such pivotal founding roles, is to be congratulated on establishing itself as a very necessary forum for discussing and communicating ideas about Freud and psychoanalysis.

At times, in the zeal or perhaps in the identification with Freud—the discoverer, the synthesizer, the translator, the creator—various individuals have attempted to found new schools, to be proclaimed as Freud's successors, to take one theoretic principle or set of clinical observations and develop what they believe to be "the new psychoanalysis." This often is followed by criticism of Freud—why did he do this, why did he say that, why did he ignore this, and so forth. In this process of criticism, the tendency is to forget, ignore, and, unfortunately in some instances, to misstate what Freud did say or, at times, to connect his name with statements he never made. Freud had an open system—he could observe himself and others, he could fashion his ideas into theoretical systems, and he could test these clinically. If they were in error or needed to be more specific than the implied universality of his initial formulation, he would modify, reexamine, and reconceptualize what he previously asserted, and when necessary even abandon a cherished idea.

Eissler now reexamines, reemphasizes, and re-creates some of Freud's contributions for those in the present generation who may not be completely familiar with Freud's work. In the brief space allotted to me for this discussion, I can focus on only one or, at best, two themes in Eissler's presentation. There is so much that is stimulated by this essay that I am hard put to choose what to highlight, but I will try to discuss some themes that emerge.

Eissler writes that "there is no finite border set for the interpretation of dreams; that is to say, the interpretation of a dream, even of a dream element, is never ended once and for all—it appears to be potentially infinite."

In dreams are our hidden history, and Daniel Boorstin, in his collection of essays on *Hidden History: Exploring Our Secret Past*, has noted that "of the several kinds of creativity, the least secret, the most public, the most discussable is *social* creativity" (1989, xv). In Eissler's paper we are sharing the evolution of the creative ideas of one of the few geniuses of the world. Freud's contributions resulted in new ways of looking at our internal and external world—new approaches, new observations, new theories, new frontiers that fueled his own creative energies and stimulated that of others. Boorstin suggests three characteristic ways of thinking and feeling that bear on this theme. First, there is an "exaggerated self-awareness." This refers to self-observation at various levels. These reflections may give rise to the second characteristic—a heightened "openness to novelty and change"; we encounter something new and different, and even if it is at variance with existing beliefs it stimulates further exploration. The third characteristic involves a strong community awareness. "In the face of the different and the unfamiliar, we, the similars, lean on one another. We seek to reassure one another as we organize our new communities and new forms of community" (Boorstin 1989, xvii).

These three characteristics of creativity present both opportunities and challenges. Sometimes contradictions appear and attempts at reconciliation involve self-criticism and disagreements with others, but this is the path of creativity, of facing the unknown, of communicating what one observes, understands, formulates. Creative dissatisfaction reminds us "not only of what we know, what we can do, but of what we do not know, what impossibilities still remain to be accomplished, or at least tried. Our task is to remain aware of these [encounters] . . . and to keep the borders open to a competitive world of new ideas, new products, new arts, new institutions" (Boorstin 1989, xxvii). Like Freud, Eissler is a discoverer and creator in his own right. He tries to study the past in depth, give us an opportunity to follow his accounts, and then reduce or if possible remove ambiguity. But this is not an easy job. Reconstructing and rediscovering the past is part of analytic work, and for the psychoanalytic historian, working with relics and derivatives that surface in the present without the original creator present to augment and fill in crucial details, the task becomes ever so difficult. One must rely on whatever one can find, think about, and understand.

What gets formulated as an explanation or version of reality can be absorbed into the unconscious and then seen as reality or truth, even if this is not true. Thus constant vigilance and scientific-clinical skepticism may be needed to buttress one's understanding of reality. As Barthes has written, "The *explanation* of a work is always sought in the man or woman who produced it, as if it were always in the end, through the more or less transparent allegory of fiction, the voice of a single person, the *author* 'confiding' in us" (as quoted in Homberger and Charmley 1988, x); and yet science involves reality testing by the individual whose ideas are examined and by the community of peer researchers-clinicians-scientists. There are other issues that may, for personal reasons, remain unwritten. "Biography is a massive socially sanctioned invasion of the privacy of private life; we have become the most voyeuristic culture in history" (p. xi). "All forms of biography have become increasingly frank about sexual activity. This is no longer a direct part of the legacy of Freud's contribution to biography . . . but a reflection of a more pervasive and diffused recognition that sex and gender are not the background of an individual's life, not the interludes, but are part of the foreground as well" (p. xii).

Freud, who shared so much of his life with us, wrote in "An Autobiographical Study" (1935): "The public has no claim to learn any more of my personal affairs. . . . I have . . . been more open and frank in some of my writings . . . than people usually are who describe their lives for their contemporaries or for posterity. I have had small thanks for it, and from my experience I cannot recommend anyone to follow my example" (p. 73). We may be curious to know from where ideas come, and we seek to correlate life and creative work; but this may still not explain the genius or creativity that possibly most interests us. Perhaps this is because we do not have all of the facts, palatable and unpalatable, or because we can never understand what is so unusual; but we still are very curious. Is it all sublimation? Are we looking for simple or reductionistic explanations? What evidence do we seek for our hypotheses? Are these diaries, letters, reports, interviews, autobiographies sufficient or authentic? These are some of the methodologic problems we confront. What has been distorted, omitted, elaborated, and left out? Disentangling legend from reality becomes another challenge. The imaginative leap beyond records at times is most valuable and here we must rely upon the biographer-historian. At times the bias or individual perspective of the biographer is critical. How do we circumvent some of these dilemmas? The psychoanalyst, by studying patterns of behavior, responses to life situations, following up on clues and connections, as Eissler does, helps us with our explanations and also with the identification of what we do not know and may never know. The observations and testing by others can be of great assistance in checking on the intuition, imagination, and formulation of the original creative thinker. We learn much about the topic under study as well as about the personal life of the creator and the biographer. We detect when the past may have been restructured, where failures, misjudgments, and errors may have been covered over for various reasons. And yet understanding unsuccessful pursuits can be of great scientific and clinical use.

Of course hindsight, where outcome is known, makes the writing of a piece of biography or history easier than when results are unknown. But here again one must examine the supposedly tight linkage between antecedents and consequents. They may not be significantly related. Assumptions must be looked at carefully. Poking and prying can be very useful, and when it involves self-examination one can see how this process can be resisted in many places.

Much more can be discussed about methodological issues as they relate to Freud and his formulations and testing of his psychoanalytic hypotheses. But now I wish to turn to Freud's preoccupation with death. Eissler calls our attention to Freud's possible guilt as it was related to the death of his brother Julius. He very plausibly suggests Freud's identification with Macbeth, Joseph, Max and Moritz; and Freud's dreams of himself as a thief and a plagiarizer may be a manifestation of his guilt. His Oedipal guilt is well documented, although his concern with longevity, fear of "penetrating into forbidden recesses," suggests that his "ideas, fears, and fantasies about death were tied to his [Freud's] exploratory activities from the beginning." Freud's fears of calamities, his exile, his many later personal losses, his painful illness—all seemed to fit in with his concerns. And yet he seemingly moved forward in his discoveries. Despite the attempts made to discredit him through deviousness, gossip, rumor, clever innuendos, he continued with his work. Like Moses, he unfortunately did not live to enter the "promised land" where his ideas, despite the painful attacks made upon him, have permeated almost all facets of man's activities.

Eissler discusses the impacts of these betrayals and malignments when he describes "a desperate mood Freud felt in old age about his final accomplishments" and about "his youthful work when as a matter of fact it was deserving of high praise." "His youthful style [methodology] had been impeccable, no less so than that of later years, and from the beginning he was loyal to the principles for whose realization he would continue to exert himself for the rest of his life: enlarging knowledge of empirical fact and endeavoring to make theoretical inferences on the highest level of abstraction." But again, as Eissler notes, "Freud was always tormented by misgivings about the future of psychoanalysis." He envisioned that psychoanalysis "would decay into schools separated irreconcilably." Perhaps, as Eissler suggests, Freud felt he should have remained in neurology where his research was so promising. In any event, we find him successful and unsuccessfully fighting off a "depression filled with remorse." Despite this chronically operative attitude and threat, he still was creative and productive in ways that few achieve. It is as if creativity were based on pain. As Eissler notes, Freud's creative outpouring never stood still. "Death was finally enforced by Freud's own decision when the body denied any pleasure and became nothing but a bucket of pain." He was aware of the "temporality of his findings and theories, but [Eissler] venture[s] to speculate that he wanted to shoot the arrow as far as possible" and that he would remodel or extend psychoanalytic knowledge further if he had lived—perhaps in the direction of a new ego psychology.

We are very grateful to Eissler for his many contributions to our field and now we can add another heartfelt thanks. We look forward to his next creative addition to our thought, our knowledge, and our ideals.

References

Boorstin, Daniel J. 1989. *Hidden History: Exploring Our Secret Past.* New York: Vantage Books.

Freud, S. 1935. Postscript. *S.E.* 20:71–74.

Homberger, E. and Charmley, J., eds. 1988. *The Troubled Fact of Biography.* New York: St. Martin's Press.

9

Reflections on Death, Phylogeny, and the Mind-Body Problem in Freud's Life and Work

Emanuel E. Garcia

The foregoing papers give ample evidence of the penetrating breadth of Freud's work, and they have managed as well to enhance our understanding of the creative process within him. In my concluding comments I would like to address several closely linked themes that have permeated these presentations, to give an aerial survey of a landscape that remains to be explored in detail.

But before I do so there is a general point I wish to make that has emerged forcefully from these contributions, namely, that although psychoanalysis may have been born in the clinic, it almost immediately left its confines to take its place not merely as a method of treatment, but as a general psychology. This occurred only because Freud possessed the diligence, fortitude, and relentless inquisitiveness to generalize, to create ever-more comprehensive theory, to push the boundaries of the known, and to seek, as far as possible, ultimate cause. Yet unlike a dreamy armchair speculator, Freud remained firmly grounded in factual observation—the clinical data of free association was always an anchor. However, he did not consider such free associative bedrock as the sole route to knowledge about the unconscious. In fact, he established a dialog between the revelations of an individual's free associations in the classical treatment, and the observations and interpretations of all other cultural and biological phenomena. When correspondences were seen to occur, for example, between a patient's confession of infantile incestuous desires and the drama of Oedipus Tyrannus, then Freud could be sure he was onto something. He asserted that unless an analyst were well acquainted with literature, mythology, cultural history and the psychology of religion, a great deal of clinical material would simply be incomprehensible (1926, 246). Similarly, without access to the data provided by the first reliable and systematic way of investigating the unconscious, the technique of free association—which Jones (1953–1957, 1:241) trenchantly calls one of the two greatest achievements of Freud's life (the other being his self-analysis)—much about man and culture can never be explicated. This mutually influential dialog, this compassing of observational data from the individual to society at large, from the clinic to the world without, is an integral part of psychoanalytic science. Albert Solnit nicely illustrates the process in his contribution, "Freud's View of Mental Health and Fate" (chapter 5).

To ensure the fertility of psychoanalysis Freud advocated the creation of an academy whose course of instruction would include the aforementioned subjects (history, literature, and so on) as well as biology, human sexuality, psychiatry, and others.

In the United States, one can escape the most prestigious schools with only a smattering of the kind and scope of knowledge obtained by Freud and his peers. Entry into an analytic institute, with or without medical training, guarantees primarily that one can emerge with a sound treatment technique, but not much else. During his training the typical candidate is already working full-time as a psychiatrist or psychotherapist—in rare cases, another profession such as anthropology, history, or linguistics—and he is not likely to have the leisure to remedy educational deficits, let alone embark on the kind of cross-fertilizing research analysis requires for its growth.

Unfortunately I do not think there has been any attempt to construct such a college along the lines recommended by Freud. Even Anna Freud's description of the ideal psychoanalytic institute falls far short of his prescription: she in fact dismisses it as a piece of " 'fantastic' wishful thinking" (A. Freud 1966, 75). However, the creative advancement of psychoanalysis may depend on the creation of such academies.

Bear in mind that Freud's development of a psychoanalytic thanatology could not have occurred without the impetus of insights derived outside the clinical setting, specifically from the works of Shakespeare and observations on the consequences of war (see Eissler 1955, 10–30). This brings me to the topic of death and its place in psychoanalytic thought.

Death and Psychoanalytic Psychology

Eissler observes in his paper, "An Interpretation of Four of Freud's Letters," (chapter 7), that Freud was possessed by a need to demonstrate to others the improbable, to reproduce and communicate the feeling he experienced when his mother astonished him as a six-year-old boy by rubbing her hands and producing indisputable evidence of human mortality. To repeat Freud's recollection:

When I was six years old and was given my first lessons by my mother, I was expected to believe that we were all made of earth and must therefore return to earth. This did not suit me and I expressed doubts of the doctrine. My mother thereupon rubbed the palms of her hands together . . . and showed me the blackish scales of *epidermis* produced by the friction as a proof that we were made of earth. My astonishment at this ocular demonstration knew no bounds and I acquiesced in the belief which I was later to hear expressed in the words: *'Du bist der Natur einen Tod schuldig.'* (Freud 1900, 205)

I wish to assert further that Freud was driven to demonstrate the actual *content* of his mother's breathtaking lesson as well, that is, the necessity of death. Amid the rich depiction of life that one finds in Freud's work, in all its sexual and emotional variety, there hovers ever-present the image of man the organism, fated to die, the prey of natural laws no less than his animal brethren.

In "The Theme of the Three Caskets" (1913b) Freud uncovered the disguised motif of man's need to make peace with death in two superficially dissimilar plays of Shakespeare, *King Lear* and the *Merchant of Venice*. A little later, in the much-neglected "Thoughts for the Times on War and Death" (1915c), Freud vehemently criticized the conventional "civilized" attitude of attempting to deny the reality of death, noting that such an attitude results in paralyzing grief when a loved one dies, and consequently a serious impoverishment of life. Freud advocated a less illusory approach, one that would permit man to tackle with exuberance the complex tasks of living. "If you want to endure life," he advised, "prepare yourself for death" (p. 300). In fact, he ascribed to primeval man's encounter with death nothing less than the very birth of psychology and culture! And in the poetic "On Transience" (1916), Freud asserts that life itself is all the more valuable for its brevity and the certainty of its end.

Beyond the Pleasure Principle (1920) marked the introduction of the concept of a death drive that unequivocally emphasized the fundamental importance of death as *the* organizing principle of organic and psychological life. It irrevocably challenged psychoanalytic psychology to account both practically and theoretically for death. Otherwise, a psychology that failed to give this central and unyielding piece of reality its rightful place as the aim of life (p. 38) could hardly claim to be comprehensive.

Those who dismiss the death drive as being clinically irrelevant or clinically unsupported (an attitude highly debatable, by the way) are missing the fundamental point that the clinic is not the sole source of data nor the *raison d'être* of psychoanalysis. The dual drive theory represented a remarkable culmination of far-ranging observation that included cell biology, clinical data, literature, and so forth. It is a theory that embraces both the organic and psychological aspects of life itself. (For a thoroughgoing exploration of the viability of the postulate of a death drive, see Eissler 1971.)

The idea of a death drive grew in a direct line of descent from Freud's early formulation of a principle of constancy. This becomes especially clear when one contrasts Josef Breuer's conceptualization of a constancy principle with Freud's. Albrecht Hirschmüller, in his biography of Breuer (1990), shows that the development of a constancy principle that was to be applied to the joint work of Breuer and Freud on hysteria became a source of fundamental disagreement (pp. 159–163). Breuer argued for a physiological process of brain regulation whose goal was to maintain an optimum but varying level of intracerebral tonic excitation. His homeostatic system allowed for increases and decreases—in short, a dynamic equilibrium. Freud, on the other hand, described a process that sought *to eliminate excitation altogether*—a "null principle" or "principle of neuronal inertia" striving for a zero state of tension, but which can be influenced by the "exigencies of life" to convert its original trend toward inertia into the secondary function of attempting to minimize and maintain constant tension (1895, 296–298). Even though Freud regarded his constancy principle to be a fundamental contribution to the theory of hysteria, it was omitted from the jointly authored "Preliminary Communication" because of Breuer's sharp disagreement (Hirschmüller 1990, 160).

Does not the early null principle uncannily foreshadow the death drive, which itself seeks to convert the living into inorganicity, and which is deflected from this aim only by fusion with Eros, the "life-preserving forces" (Freud 1920, 49)? Here is an example of how intimations of an idea had lain in embryo for decades before finally emerging as a more comprehensive entity. Eventually Freud would describe the constancy principle (now called the Nirvana principle) as a derivative of the death drive, and to distinguish the pleasure principle from it as a modification caused by the "life instinct," libido (1924, 160).

One may object that Freud in 1893 went far beyond the evidence available to him to formulate such an extreme idea, so defiant of common sense, particularly in light of Breuer's much more practicable and sensible notion of dynamic homeostasis. The story of Breuer and Freud is, however, one of an extraordinarily gifted talent and a genius. It is precisely in their differences that we may be permitted a glimpse into the forces that propel the genius and set him apart from the near-great. Freud's indomitable tendency to see beyond the immediate, to bring to light transcendent, universal mental phenomena is much evident, not only in his views on constancy, but also in his dissatisfaction with Breuer's hypnoid states and his attempt to generalize the concept of defense to all of hysteria (Breuer and Freud, 1893–1895, 286).

But to return to the death drive. Again, at the time of the *Stud-*

ies, there can be little doubt that notwithstanding its physiologic fetters, Breuer's version of the constancy principle was much more parsimoniously in keeping with clinical observation; Freud's strained at the bit. Even Freud's final comprehensive elaboration of the death drive has remained refractory to assimilation by most, in part because it was described as working silently, manifesting itself indirectly, and also because it is highly disturbing to acknowledge the presence of a malignant force at work within whose constant and only goal is to render one lifeless. It would not be the first time, however, that a genius defied common sense or adhered to ideas despite apparently sensible refutations and contradictions. Darwin, for example, weathered compellingly logical attacks on his theory of natural selection, only to be vindicated in the end (Vorzimmer 1970).

An anecdote related by a prominent physicist writing about Einstein seems to sum up the prevailing attitude toward Freud's death drive: a graduate of the California Institute of Technology was told by his professor, a famous astronomer, that he should under no circumstances consider working in general relativity, because it "had so little connection with the rest of physics and astronomy" (Will 1986). The death drive, which seems to many to have so little connection with psychoanalytic practice and theory, may yet be recognized as an essential part of psychoanalysis, the way general relativity has come to assume its pivotal place in physics and astronomy.

The Phylogenetic Viewpoint

This leads us to another of the controversial topics whose value Robert A. Paul emphasizes in chapter 1, "Freud's Anthropology," namely, the evolutionary history of man and its relation to his present-day psychology. As the recent publication of Freud's lost metapsychological summary paper, the "Overview of the Transferences Neuroses" (1987) attests, phylogeny was indeed a central concern of Freud's and was implicated by him in his investigations of a variety of phenomena: drives and defenses, sexuality, the latency period, and the Oedipus complex; id, ego, and superego development; the formation of memories and fantasies; religion, culture, symbolism, and dreaming; and the etiology of neuroses and psychoses (see Garcia 1988). In his obituary of Ferenczi (1933), he praised Ferenczi's application of analysis to evolutionary biology, *Thalassa,* with the following words:

This little book is a biological rather than a psycho-analytic study; it is an application of the attitudes and insights associated with psycho-analysis to the biology of the sexual processes and, beyond them, to organic life in general. It was perhaps the boldest application of psychoanalysis that was ever attempted. As its governing thought it lays stress on the conservative nature of the instincts, which seek to re-establish every state of things that has been abandoned owing to an external interference. Symbols are recognized as evidence of ancient connections. Impressive instances are adduced to show how the characteristics of what is psychical preserve traces of primaeval changes in the bodily substance. When one has read this work, one seems to understand many peculiarities of sexual life of which one had never previously been able to obtain a comprehensive view, and one finds oneself the richer for hints that promise a deep insight into wide fields of biology. It is a vain task to attempt already today to distinguish what can be accepted as an authentic discovery from what seeks, in the fashion of a scientific phantasy, to guess at future knowledge. (p. 228)

I have quoted this passage at such length because it shows clearly Freud's serious and abiding interest in this kind of application of analysis, and because these words with little modification might have been written about his own *Totem and Taboo,* the *Overview,* and other phylogenetically flavored writings.

Whether or not one accepts Freud's literal construction of events in *Totem and Taboo*—the murder and cannibalistic incorporation of the primal horde's father by his sons—one must at least acknowledge that here Freud was on his typically relentless search for origins, strenuously attempting to account for the evolution and persistence of indisputable psychological facts. Dr. Paul considers moot the question of literal historicity, and I should like to remind readers that Freud himself offered a persuasive argument against the necessity of literal construction. But Freud rejected this argument, insisting on the distinction between psychical and external reality, thought and deed, notwithstanding the "omnipotence of thought" that characterizes the thinking of primeval man, neurotics, and children:

If wishes and impulses have the full value of facts for primitive men, it is our business to give their attitude our understanding attention instead of correcting it in accordance with our own standards. Let us, then, examine more closely the case of neurosis—comparisons with which led us into our present uncertainty. It is not accurate to say that obsessional neurotics, weighed down under the burden of an excessive morality, are defending themselves only against *psychical* reality and are punishing themselves for impulses which were merely *felt*. *Historical* reality has a share in the matter as well. In their childhood they had these evil impulses pure and simple, and turned them into acts so far as the impotence of childhood allowed. . . . The analogy between primitive men and neurotics will therefore be far more fully established if we suppose that in the former instance, too, psychical reality—as to the form taken by which we are in no doubt— coincided at the beginning with factual reality: that primitive men actually *did* what all the evidence shows that they intended to do. (Freud 1913a, 160–161).

We need not believe in a one-to-one correspondence between the history of early man and present-day childhood for the above to be accepted, only that certain parallels do exist between childhood thought, the cultural practices of "primitive" tribes, and the ways of prehistoric man—a reasonable assumption in my view. (It is noteworthy that Freud was well aware of the distinctions between so-called present-day primitives and true primeval man [1913a, 161; 1915c, 295)]).

The progress of civilization can been as an increasingly successful attempt to dispel the illusions of primary-process thinking—by relinquishing magic for science, by sacrificing more for less illusory understandings of the world, of which the psyche is a part. Freud believed that for primitive man, thought passed directly into action, that in the beginning truly was the Deed. This is the sticking point.

The Museum of the Ancient Orient in Istanbul has on display a Babylonian clay tablet inscribed with a portion of Hammurabi's code. Law 157 reads: "If a man has lain in the bosom of his mother after the death of his father, they [mother and son] shall both be burnt to death as punishment." Such legislation was stimulated by the fact that the Oedipal crime must have been perpetrated in action, not mere fantasy. Given the well-documented historical evidence for parricide, castration, and cannibalism among "not-so-premeval" men, in conjunction with the frank and ubiquitous mythological representations of such practices (which Lawrence

M. Siegel [1989] has meticulously described), some version of Freud's scenario seems highly probable.

It is worthwhile juxtaposing these assumptions with Freud's comments not long after *Totem* was written, in the paper on war and death (1915c). There I think is an important addition to his ideas about the omnipotence of thought, the equation of deed and thought, and the birth of self-reflection. Freud saw the division of body and soul as a result of primeval man's ambivalence in the face of the death of a loved (and hated) person—wife, child, friend. Thus,

Man could no longer keep death at a distance, for he had tasted it in his pain about the dead; but he was nevertheless unwilling to acknowledge it, for he could not conceive of himself as dead. So he devised a compromise: he conceded the fact of his own death as well, but denied it the significance of annihilation—a significance which he had had no motive for denying where the death of his enemy was concerned. It was beside the dead body of someone he loved that he invented spirits, and his sense of guilt at the satisfaction mingled with his sorrow turned these new-born spirits into evil demons that had to be dreaded. (1915c, 294)

If one accepts that an awareness of death is the hallmark of the human species, then we owe nothing less than the birth of culture to its influence, and can discern its intimate connections with reflection, the interposition of thought between impulse and action.

There is another feature of Freud's phylogenetic preoccupation that bears mentioning. Clinically he did not invoke phylogeny to explain anything until he had exhausted all other avenues of understanding. Nor did he rely on phylogeny to diminish individual responsibility or minimize the developmental experiences of infantile sexuality, as did Jung when he retreated into the mystical realm of a collective unconscious. In the case history of the Wolf Man, Freud fell back on a phylogenetic explanation only as a last resort. He could not account for his patient's identification of his father as castrating figure from the clinical material, because it was strictly from women that the Wolf-man had reported receiving castration threats (1918, 88). Freud considered the introduction of phylogenetic constructions to be admissible only "when psychoanalysis strictly observes the correct order of precedence, and, after forcing its way through the strata of what has been acquired by the individual, comes at last upon traces of what has been inherited" (1918, 121).

It is noteworthy that in one of his early neurohistologic researches, on the primitive fish Petromyzon in 1878, he made a solid empirical contribution to the theory of evolution by demonstrating the continuity between cells of the nervous system of a primitive animal with those of higher vertebrates (Jones 1953–1957, 1:48, 219). The parallels between such early studies and his later psychological work are unmistakable. In summary, Freud envisioned man in a Darwinian context, one species among many, whose physical *and mental* characteristics had been molded by evolutionary forces. Thus the phylogenetic endowment of the psyche, which constitutes a "nucleus of the unconscious" (1918, 120), is a legitimate area of psychoanalytic investigation.

I am happy to report that this aspect of Freud's work has been gaining increasing attention (see Grubrich-Simitis 1987, 1988) and that a synthesis of analytic ideas with sociobiology is being attempted (see Badcock 1990a, 1990b). However, I believe that a profitable emphasis of such research would be placed not so much on questions about the Oedipus complex per se as an evolutionary adaptation, but on an examination of the mental mechanisms Freud revealed to be universal constituents of the psychic apparatus—condensation, displacement, projection, symbolism, the production of anxiety, overdetermination, and so forth. Which evolutionary circumstances may have given rise to these phenomena? How might they have contributed to the species' survival? The Wolf Man's identification of his father as castrator may be more a result of a phylogenetically timed projection rather than an inherited memory. In other words, given a set of phylogenetically programmed processes that unfold in a specific developmental sequence, the child is destined to react in relatively predictable ways to his environment, and the Oedipus complex is an inevitable outcome. This would help to explain why in settings and cultures much different from Western nuclear families, the Oedipus complex takes on different forms. A phyletic history of such characteristics of mental functioning would make for a fascinating study, and it is to be hoped that a satisfactory integration of human ethology with psychoanalysis will soon be accomplished.

The Mind-Body Dilemma

The so-called mind-body problem has puzzled mankind for centuries. It seems that neither the monistic nor dualistic version of this age-old enigma offers a satisfying solution. Somehow the mind and body are separate, yet somehow they are inextricably connected, beginning with the assumption that without the body the mind cannot exist. But when we acknowledge to ourselves the power of mind over soma, we plunge into a tangle of baffling complexities. No wonder that this problem has occupied philosophers and physicians for so long.

Freud was greatly intrigued in this subject, and were it not for the dramatic displays of the mind's action on the body in hysteria, he might never have trodden the analytic path. Charcot's hypnotic induction of hysterical paralyses and the resolution of Anna O.'s conversion symptoms deeply impressed him. As early as 1893 he devoted a paper to distinguishing between organic and hysterical motor paralyses (Freud 1893). But even earlier, in 1890, he had written a work to which may be traced many of the tenets of modern psychosomatic medicine (Freud 1890). In "Psychical (or Mental) Treatment" he asserted that all mental states have physical manifestations and are capable of modifying somatic processes (Freud 1890, 287–288). He catalogued the physical changes caused by persistent affective conditions such as depression, including undernourishment, or "morbid changes" in the walls of blood vessels. He commented on the influence of emotions on the ability to resist infection, claimed that depression could significantly shorten the lifespan, and that a deep humiliation or disgrace could end life suddenly. He gave credence to "miracle cures," taking care to note that bona fide organic illnesses could be remedied through the operation of strictly psychological forces. Indeed, Freud implied that the power of the physician's personality and authority (that is, transference) has this very capability.

Although there is no bibliography attached to Freud's article (which appeared in *Die Gesundheit*, a collection of medical essays for a popular audience), I am fairly certain that Freud relied on a little-known work by Daniel Hack Tuke entitled "Illustrations of the Influence of the Mind upon the Body in Health and Disease"

(1884) as a source for his assertions. Freud owned a copy of Tuke's volume, which bore his personal stamp (see Eissler 1979). The many points of correspondence between it and his article leave little doubt about its usefulness to Freud. (I am currently engaged in an investigation of the nature and extent of Tuke's influence on Freud's contribution.)

Why Freud did not continue working in this particular vein makes for an interesting biographical question. He certainly did not lose interest in this type of psychosomatic approach, as his appreciation of Georg Groddeck attests. Groddeck, the "wild analyst" who made his way to psychoanalysis through the practice of general medicine, is considered a founder of psychosomatic medicine (see Grossman and Grossman, 1965). Groddeck scorned to distinguish between mental and physical illness and reported extraordinary examples of the psychotherapeutic cure of organic conditions such as retinal hemorrhages, phlebitis, goiter, scleroderma, chronic inflammation, and others (Groddeck 1977). He audaciously proclaimed that "limiting psychoanalytical treatment to the field of neurosis does not give enough knowledge of the workings of analysis. . . . Psychoanalysis may not and will not stop before organic suffering. How far its power will extend we shall see" (quoted in Grossman and Grossman 1965, 83).

Freud admired and encouraged Groddeck's work, hesitating only before the mystical and philosophical strain that leaped to the fore from time to time (see the Freud-Groddeck correspondence in Groddeck 1977). And Groddeck's name is invoked by Freud in a fateful context, to be related below.

Reciprocally, the body's influence on the mind is a theme of vast importance throughout Freud's research, and it may be summed up by a sentence in the dreambook which states that all psychic activity is ultimately derived from somatic (sensory) stimuli, internal or external (1900, 537). Freud's entire psychoanalytic output may be considered to be an immensely complex elaboration of this principle. In this context he held two opinions firmly all his life: that mind could not exist without brain, and that "physical processes must precede psychical ones' (Jones 1953–1957, 1:368).

This brings us to the period in Freud's education when he studied with Theodor Meynert, which Albrecht Hirschmüller has so ably described in chapter 3, "Freud at Meynert's Clinic." Although Meynert's neuroanatomic approach to the mind appears woefully sterile to us now, we should keep in mind that Freud spoke of "the great Meynert, in whose footsteps I had trodden with such deep veneration" (1900, 437), and always remembered Meynert as "the most brilliant genius he had ever encountered" (Jones 1953–1957, 1:65). These comments were made in spite of the fact that Meynert had become quite hostile to Freud, so there must have been something potently attractive to him about Meynert's neuroanatomic endeavors.

The *Project for a Scientific Psychology* (Freud 1895) bears this out. Whatever else the *Project* is, it is certainly a most difficult work. I believe it is inadequate to describe it as a purely psychological account clothed in the language of neurology. It seems both fish and fowl—at some points clearly psychological, but at others a literal attempt to elucidate specific neurophysiologic processes responsible for psychical acts.

Obviously the mind-body problem in all of its many ramifications is an enormous one, comprising the relations of brain tissue to psychical activities, the effect of thought and emotion on somatic functioning, the distinction between organic and psychologically caused physical disorders, and so forth. Freud never seemed to have abandoned the hope of correlating somatic with psychical activity, and he clearly remained fascinated by the mind-body issue throughout his career. His description of the drives as lying on the frontier between somatic and mental process. (1915a, 121–122), his struggle with the problem of anxiety, where the intersection between bodily and mental domains cannot be more evident (1926a), and references to hysterical conversion as an incomprehensible mystery (1909, 157) all attest to an enduring interest.

In this general context, it is noteworthy that Freud probably misdiagnosed an oral lesion that led ultimately to the cancer that caused him so much suffering and eventually killed him. Writing to Ferenczi on 6 November 1917, Freud announced the appearance of a painful swelling of the palate which he thought had worsened since he had quit his beloved cigar smoking. He reported: "Then a patient brought me fifty cigars, I lit one, became cheerful, and the affection of the palate rapidly went down. I should not have believed it had it not been so striking. Quite à la Groddeck" (quoted in Jones 1953–1957, 2:192).

It is hard to understand how Freud could have attributed to the *cessation* of smoking the development of a precancerous lesion, and would have assumed that the resumption of smoking would cure it (see Schur 1972, 310). Freud prided himself on differential diagnosis, and his practice demanded the accurate distinction of organic from functional disorders. In his discussion of the famous Irma dream, French called the fear that he had missed an organic illness "a perpetual source of anxiety to a specialist whose practice is almost limited to neurotic patients and who is in the habit of attributing to hysteria a great number of symptoms which other physicians treated as organic" (1900, 109). The illogicality of his self-diagnostic reasoning points to some deep-rooted phenomenon: perhaps it was Freud's way of unconsciously providing for himself the "constantly activated fear of being close to death," which Eissler suggests was so essential to his creativity, and which I will take up again below.

Death and Freud's Personal Development

Goethe's childhood was permeated by the exposure to the deaths of family members. Freud's early years were also touched by death: at the age of nineteen months his eight-month-old brother Julius died (Freud 1985, 268; Jones, 1953–1957, 1:7). The specific influences of experiences of death on the lives of the great has yet to be adequately explored, but there is circumstantial evidence to indicated that such experiences might well be crucial to the development of genius.

It is remarkable to observe how death was linked to various turning points in Freud's life. In the summer of 1883 Freud was shocked to learn of the suicide of a friend and colleague, the neurologist Nathan Weiss. Jones asserts that Weiss's death "emboldened Freud to decide on a neurological career in his place" (Jones 1953–1957, 1:166)—certainly an important step. In the 1908 preface to the second edition of the *Interpretation of Dreams*, Freud described his revolutionary masterwork as a reaction to his father's death (1900, xxvi); to Fliess he had written that his father's death had reawakened the entire past for him in his inner self (letter of 2 November 1896, in Freud 1985, 202). Even Freud's belief in the genuineness of hypnotic phenomena seemed predicated on intimations of mortality. In a scene recalling his mother's "dust to dust" demonstration, Freud's acceptance of the effects of hypnosis was sealed only when the magnetist Hansen brought a subject seemingly close to death (Jones 1953–1957, 1: 235).

An Addition to the Gisela Fluss Episode

Much earlier Freud had tasted death in a different way in conjunction with an episode that had profoundly altered his life's course. I am referring to the time when the sixteen-year-old Freud fell powerfully in love with Gisela Fluss while visiting his birthplace in 1872. This episode has been discussed in detail by Dr. Eissler (1978), who makes a convincing case for its pivotal importance in the development of Freud's life course. In brief, the young Freud became acutely infatuated with the dark-haired, dark-eyed girl during his sojourn to Freiberg. Gisela, however, left town after a few days, and Freud had not been able to declare his affection beforehand (Jones) 1953–1957, 1:25. His sexual desires were raised to a pitch of almost unbearable intensity, and he coped with them in a variety of defensive ways. He poured hostility upon the object of his desires, going to far as to christen his beloved with the derogatory nickname "Ichthyosaura." He adopted a puritanical attitude toward normal adolescent erotism and warned his youthful friend Eduard Silberstein not to kiss, while he himself shunned girls. He devoted himself single-mindedly to academic studies, and the direction of his work was fatefully altered away from the humanities, so dear to his heart, and toward medicine.

With the recent publication of the Freud-Silberstein correspondence (Freud 1990), additional details have come to light. It seems that Freud transferred his affection for Gisela toward her mother, writing in glowing terms of the older woman's virtues (letter of 4 September 1872, in Freud 1990, 14–19). Although it is tempting to interpret these sentiments, and indeed the love for Gisela, simply as a manifestation of Oedipal desires, of whom Gisela's mother was the principal substitute for Freud's own mother, this does not lead us very far, and furthermore detracts from what I think is the defensive use of a pseudo-Oedipal screen against the violent adolescent infatuation—a phenomenon that is common in adolescence, but perhaps not often emphasized.

In this context an ominous incident has been revealed, and I owe thanks to Dr. Eissler for directing my attention to it. Shortly after Gisela's departure, the forlorn Freud confessed the following to Siblerstein: "I had a terrible attack of toothache. I was raving the whole day, and having tried every remedy in vain, *I took some pure alcohol* to deaden the pain. . . . I soon fell asleep, or rather, passed out. Emil [Gisela's brother] had me taken upstairs, the severe shock on an empty stomach did the rest; I vomited violently but lost the toothache as I'd wanted" (letter of 4 September 1872, in Freud 1990, 18; my italics).

Any doubt that this incident was linked to Freud's infatuation with Gisela is dispelled by his reference in the same letter to Gisela's wild beauty, his admission that her image haunted him, and a postscript that reminded Silberstein of the ostensible *lack* of a connection between Gisela's departure and his illness (surely an unnecessary comment that only reveals the opposite).

The passage and the event it describes are enigmatic. Was the "toothache" a cryptic reference to unbearable sexual excitement, or to masturbation? Freud wrote that in males dreams with a dental stimulus were derived from "nothing other than masturbatory desires of the pubertal period" (1900 385), that the interpretation of dreams with a dental stimulus as dreams of masturbation was correct beyond a doubt (p. 387), and that the tooth was a frequent symbol for the male genital (pp. 357, 385–397). He explicitly links toothache and masturbation in his notes to the Rat-Man Case (1909, 269). And one can ask, what kind of toothache can be cured by pure alcohol? Did the adolescent succumb to autoerotic temptation only to punish himself by an unconscious attempt at suicide via ingestion of a dangerous substance?

The Gisela affair caused a grave upheaval in Freud's emotional state and led to an uncharacteristically dangerous example of acting out—a symbolic attempt at suicide no less. Thus, once again the specter of death rises at a crucial point in Freud's life, and we witness Freud drastically attempting to quell the riot of unruly erotic feelings by a sort of personal anticipatory enactment of the processes he would describe in his constancy principle and death drive, the reduction of tension to a zero state.

I fear I may have led readers far afield with these speculations, but nevertheless I believe they may be integrated with Dr. Eissler's description of Freud's longing for the halcyon days of neurohistologic research—research that was performed on the descendants of Ichthyosauri and the equivalent of the epidermal scales with which his mother had indelibly astonished him.

Death and the Perceptual Apparatus

By way of introduction to this section, allow me to refer to an autobiographical passage from Dostoyevsky's *The Idiot*, which may contain the key to an understanding of a facet of genius. In it Prince Myshkin related the experiences of a young man sentenced to be executed, only to have the sentence withdrawn and his life spared at the last minute. In the interval between the sentence and the pardon, some twenty minutes, the poor man felt as if an eternity of time stretched before him. His memory of the most minute details of the episode remained extraordinarily vivid, and his "last" moments were plagued by the incessant idea that if he were granted life he would be granted eternity: each minute would be a century. Such a precious commodity as time would never again be squandered.

The awareness of one's death seems to foster an enhanced perceptual appreciation of the environment in the context of slowly passing time. For the genius, psychological time seems to take on the dilatory qualities described by Dostoyevsky. It is as if only under the pressure of death can man bring the full power of his faculties to bear on the appreciation of the world around him. The genius's extraordinary perceptual and interpretive endowment, which permits him to extract a maximum of information from his surroundings, to see that which is invisible to others (like the "dust" to which we all return!), may well be related to the special influence exerted by death on the development of his personality.

In this light, Freud's quirky numerological obsession with the year of his death (Schur 1972, 301) and the suffering he required to be productive can be interpreted as attempts to keep death near so that the creative spark might emerge. Like Mozart, who wrote that he never retired without reflecting on the possibility of not waking to see another day (Eissler 1955, 98–99), Freud kept death—consciously and unconsciously—a constant companion.

Finally, I would like to return to Freud's memory of his mother's demonstration of mortality, and apply Dr. Eissler's technique of unrestricted exegesis. The incident Freud described seems to have left many traces. He essentially devoted his life to making the invisible unconscious visible to an incredulous age. And in his diligent dissection of hundreds of eels as a youthful student, in his obsession with the "single fact," in his hours of concentration on Michelangelo's sculpture of Moses, in his descriptions of Charcot's (and his own) method of staring at facts over and over until they spoke—can we not discern the astonished six-year-old trying to come to grips with life's great mystery? His characteristic manner of working with an intense scrutiny that seemed to suspend the constraints of time bears the direct imprint of his boundless childhood initiation into the most implacable of realities.

Conclusion

Allow me to return to Freud's citation of Copernicus, Darwin, and Weyer as authors of the three greatest scientific works (1907, 245). Freud made other references to Copernicus and Darwin and linked them with the effect of psychoanalysis in subverting human megalomania, delivering wounding blows to mankind's narcissism (1916–1917, 284; 1917, 140; 1925, 221). Thus in Freud's mind the essence of great or "paradigmatic" scientific achievement lay in the ability to minimize narcissistic inteference in the evaluation of nature. Which is why he cited Darwin's *Descent of Man,* and not the *Origin of Species* in his letter to Heller (1907, 245)—a very curious choice given the latter's commonly acknowledged supremacy. This feature is also underscored by his comment in reference to the Wolf Man's case study that the more thorough the elimination of preexisting convictions, the more one would be enabled to discover (1918, 12). In the context of the reduction of narcissism, Freud spoke of the dangers of a psychoanalyst's projection of "the peculiarities of his own personality, which he has dimly perceived, into the field of science, as a theory having universal validity" (1912, 117), a statement that can be broadly applied to the general scientist.

All scientific ideas spring from the soil of one's personality. Their validity cannot be disputed on the basis of their provenance but is a question of independent verification. But the quest for knowledge is marked by a fundamental paradox: man's understanding of his environment is both based upon and limited by the narcissistic projection of what has come to be assimilated by his psyche. Darwin's comparison of the role and function of natural selection to the familiar work of the animal breeder is a case in point. Freud illustrated this paradox when he discussed the development of the idea of consciousness:

(. . . without any special reflection we attribute to everyone else our own constitution and therefore our consciousness as well, and that this identification is a *sine qua non* of our understanding.) This inference (or this identification) was formerly extended by the ego to other human beings, to animals, plants, inanimate objects and to the world at large, and proved serviceable so long as their similarity to the individual ego was overwhelmingly great; but it becomes more untrustworthy in proportion as the difference between the ego and these "others" widened. (1915b, 169)

This is the basic problem in the history of science. The understanding of nature will always be subject to narcissistic distortion and consequently limited. Even when cultural evolution and the development of technology grant access into realms lying beyond the immediate world of our senses, the results will always be filtered through distinctly human sensory faculties. Thus in discussing the origin of the universe, an appeal to "anthropic" principles needs to be made (Hawking 1988, 123–124). This is not to say that limited knowledge cannot be immensely productive but only to emphasize the psychological constraints that necessarily influence perception.

Psychoanalysis occupies a very peculiar position among the general sciences. Other sciences compensate for the painful perturbations that initially occur when new discoveries shake the status quo by providing a demonstrably greater mastery over the natural world. Although Newton's laws of motion and Einstein's theory of general relativity were deeply troubling when first introduced, shattering the commonly accepted perception of the world at their respective times, they soon made possible predictive and technological feats that had been hitherto undreamed. In general, scientific advancements foster the illusion of omnipotence and immortality by granting man additional powers over his world, powers that seem to allow him to transcend the constraints of nature, as recent developments in genetics, chemistry, and physics so easily show.

Psychoanalysis, however, does nothing comparable. Instead of omnipotence it serves up reality—the inevitability of death and the horrors of infantile sexuality. Nevertheless, even in our immensely confusing times, homage to reality, no matter how stark or implacable, cannot be surpassed as a basis for constructive action, for a harmonious integration into the world around us of fellow men and natural forces. This is the foundation upon which psychoanalysis has been built, and for which Freud braved so many inner and outer dangers, sacrificing contentment for conflict, relinquishing the narrow search for certainty to embark on a quest for knowledge. Where others succumb to the tempting allurements of majestically one-dimensional psychologies, Freud stands fast in deference to complexity. The intricate depth of the human psyche demands nothing less.

References

Badcock, C. R. 1990a. *Oedipus in Evolution: A New Theory of Sex*. Oxford and Cambridge, Mass.: Basil Blackwell.

———. 1990b. Is the Oedipus complex a Darwinian adaptation? *J. American Academy of Psychoanalysis* 18:368–377.

Breuer, J., and Freud, S. 1893–1895. Studies on hysteria. *S.E.* 2:1–305.

Eissler, K. R. 1955. *The Psychiatrist and the Dying Patient*. New York: International Universities Press.

———. 1971. Death drive, ambivalence and narcissism. *Psychoanalytic Study of the Child* 26:25–78.

———. 1978. Creativity and adolescence: The effect of trauma in Freud's adolescence. *Psychoanalytic Study of the Child* 33:461–517.

———. 1979. Bericht über die sich in den Vereinigten Staaten befindenden Bücher aus S. Freuds Bibliothek. *Jahrbuch der Psychoanalyse* 11:10–50.

Ferenczi, S. 1938. *Thalassa: A Theory of Genitality*. Trans. H. A. Bunker. New York: Psychoanalytic Quarterly, Inc.

162 *Emanuel E. Garcia*

Freud, A. 1966. The ideal psychoanalytic institute: A utopia. In *The Writings of Anna Freud*, vol. 7, 73–93. New York: International Universities Press.

Freud, S. 1890. Psychical (or mental) treatment. *S.E.* 7:283–302.

_____. 1893. Some points for a comparative study of organic and hysterical motor paralyses. *S.E.* 1:160–172.

_____. 1895. Project for a scientific psychology. *S.E.* 1:295–387.

_____. 1900. The interpretation of dreams. *S.E.* 4 and 5.

_____. 1907. Contributions to a questionnaire on reading. *S.E.* 9:245–247.

_____. 1909. Notes upon a case of obsessional neurosis. *S.E.* 10:155–318.

_____. 1912. Recommendations to physicians practising psycho-analysis. *S.E.* 12:111–120.

_____. 1913a. Totem and taboo. *S.E.* 13:1–161.

_____. 1913b. The theme of the three caskets. *S.E.* 12:291–301.

_____. 1915a. Instincts and their vicissitudes. *S.E.* 14:117–140.

_____. 1915b. The unconscious. *S.E.* 14:166–204.

_____. 1915c. Thoughts for the times on war and death. *S.E.* 14:275–300.

_____. 1916. On transience. *S.E.* 14:305–307.

_____. 1916–1917. Introductory lectures on psycho-analysis. *S.E.* 15 and 16.

_____. 1917. A difficulty in the path of psycho-analysis. *S.E.* 17:137–144.

_____. 1918. From the history of an infantile neurosis. *S.E.* 17:7–122.

_____. 1920. Beyond the pleasure principle. *S.E.* 18:7–64.

_____. 1924. The economic problem of masochism. *S.E.* 19:159–170.

_____. 1925. The resistances to psycho-analysis. *S.E.* 19:213–222.

_____. 1926a. Inhibitions, symptoms and anxiety. *S.E.* 20:87–172.

_____. 1926b. The question of lay analysis. *S.E.* 20:183–258.

_____. 1933. Sandor Ferenczi. *S.E.* 22:227–229.

_____. 1985. *The Complete Letters of Sigmund Freud to Wilhelm Fliess, 1887–1904.* Ed. and trans. J. M. Masson. Cambridge, Mass.: Harvard University Press.

_____. 1987. *A Phylogenetic Fantasy* [Overview of the Transference Neuroses]. Ed. I. Grubrich-Simitis, trans. A. Hoffer and P. T. Hoffer. Cambridge, Mass.: Harvard University Press.

_____. 1990. *The Letters of Sigmund Freud to Eduard Silberstein, 1871–1881.* Ed. W. Boehlich, trans. A. J. Pomerans. Cambridge, Mass.: Harvard University Press.

Garcia, E. E. 1988. In the beginning . . . Phylogeny in Freud's *Overview of the Transference Neuroses:* A review-essay. *Jefferson Journal of Psychiatry* 6(2):89–99.

Groddeck, G. 1977. *The Meaning of Illness: Selected Psychoanalytic Writings.* New York: International Universities Press.

Grossman, C. M., and Grossman, S. 1965. *The Wild Analyst: The Life and Work of Georg Groddeck.* New York: George Braziller.

Grubrich-Simitis, I. 1987. Metapsychology and metabiology. In S. Freud, *A Phylogenetic Fantasy*, ed. I. Grubrich-Simitis, trans. A. Hoffer and P. T. Hoffer. Cambridge, Mass.: Harvard University Press.

————. 1988. Trauma or drive—drive and trauma: A reading of Sigmund Freud's Phylogenetic Fantasy of 1915. *Psychoanalytic Study of the Child* 42:3–32.

Hawking, S. W. 1988. *A Brief History of Time*. New York: Bantam Books.

Hirschmüller, A. 1990. *The Life and Work of Josef Breuer: Physiology and Psychoanalysis*. New York and London: New York University Press.

Jones, E. 1953–1957. *The Life and Work of Sigmund Freud*. 3 vols. New York: Basic Books.

Schur, M. 1972. *Freud: Living and Dying*. New York International Universities Press.

Siegel, L. M. 1989. The beginning of so many things. Unpublished manuscript.

Tuke, D. H. 1884. *Illustrations of the Influence of the Mind upon the Body in Health and Disease Designed to Elucidate the Action of the Imagination*. 2 vols. London: J. and A. Churchill.

Vorzimmer, P. J. 1970. *Charles Darwin: The Years of Controversy*. Philadelphia: Temple University Press.

Will, C. M. 1986. *Was Einstein Right? Putting General Relativity to the Test*. New York: Basic Books.

Index